Italy's Alpine Lakes

*Small-town Itineraries for
the Foodie Traveler*

Zeneba Bowers
Matt Walker

Note: Since this is a "Kindle MatchBook" you can download the Amazon Kindle for free, along with any updates, delivered automatically.

Italy's Alpine Lakes
Small-town Itineraries for the Foodie Traveler

Zeneba Bowers & Matt Walker

F I R S T   E D I T I O N

ISBN: 978-1-948018-37-1
Library of Congress Control Number: 2018959328

Copyright © 2018 Little Roads Europe, LLC
All rights reserved.

All photography by Zeneba Bowers and Matt Walker.
Maps by Laura Atkinson. Book design by Nancy Cleary. Copy edited by Kristin Whittlesey.

No portion of this book may be reproduced in any manner without the express written permission of the publisher, except for the use of quotations in a book review.

Although the authors and publisher have made every effort to ensure that the information in this book was correct at the time of publication, neither the authors nor Little Roads LLC assume any liability to any party for any loss, damage, or disruption caused by errors or omissions.

Little Roads Publishing
An Imprint of Wyatt-MacKenzie

www.LittleRoadsEurope.com

ADVANCE REVIEWS

"Little Roads' itinerary service far exceeded our expectations. The attention to detail in the planning process and the itinerary equipped us to feel like locals not tourists. Our children, ages 10 and 12, loved the freedom to explore and become immersed in the culture. As parents, we were able to relax and enjoy every moment anxiety-free. We are already talking about next summer's adventure!"

— **Peter Klassen**, Little Roads Itinerary client

"Peace, authenticity and timelessness—the perfect travel philosophy."

— **Catherine Marien**, founder of "Slow Italy"

"Conveys the real Italy, the day-to-day routines of its people and the tastes of its culinary traditions. They deliver what every armchair traveler and guidebook devotee is seeking: An indelible sense of place and the locals-only advice you need to experience it for yourself."

— **Robert Firpo-Cappiello**, Editor in Chief, *Budget Travel Magazine* (BudgetTravel.com)

"An indispensable travel companion for first timers, a must for regulars and, for the amount of golden nuggets and heaps of cherished information contained, vital for the downright lunatic Italophiles."

— **Dario Castagno**, author of *Too Much Tuscan Sun*

"This is the book that doesn't exist anywhere else. It won't just round up the usual travel suspects, information you can find anywhere. It will ferret out the places locals love, the pubs and inns and jaw-dropping sights that you might blow right past if you didn't know better."

— **Leslie Dixon**, screenwriter, *Mrs. Doubtfire, Thomas Crown Affair, Limitless*

Table of Contents

Map of Italy v
Our Goals viii
About this Book ix
Introduction xiii

ROUTE #1 1
Lago d'Orta and West Lago Maggiore

ROUTE #2 31
East Lago Maggiore and Lago di Varese

ROUTE #3 51
Lago di Como

ROUTE #4 77
Lago d'Iseo

ROUTE #5 101
Lago di Garda

ROUTE #6 121
The Trentino

ROUTE #7 145
Around Milan-Malpensa Airport

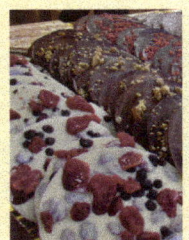
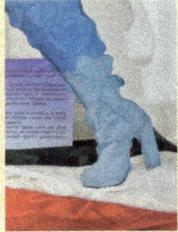

Appendix 151

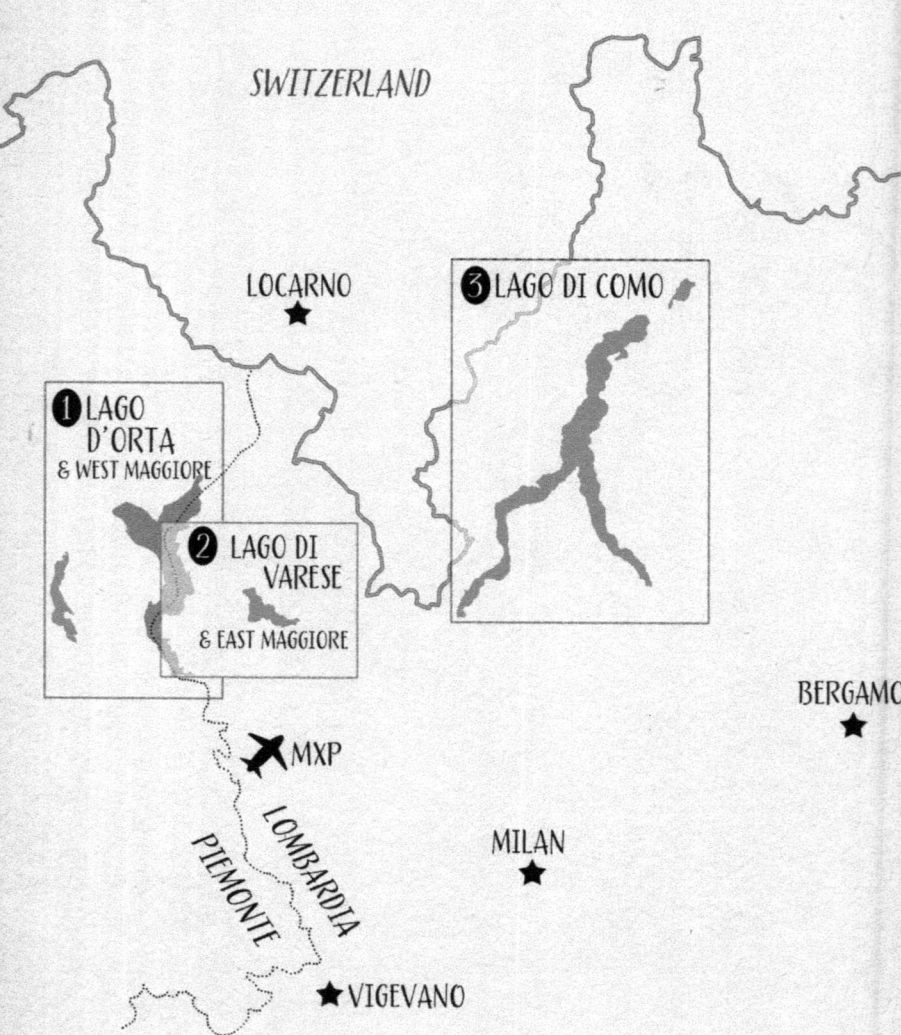

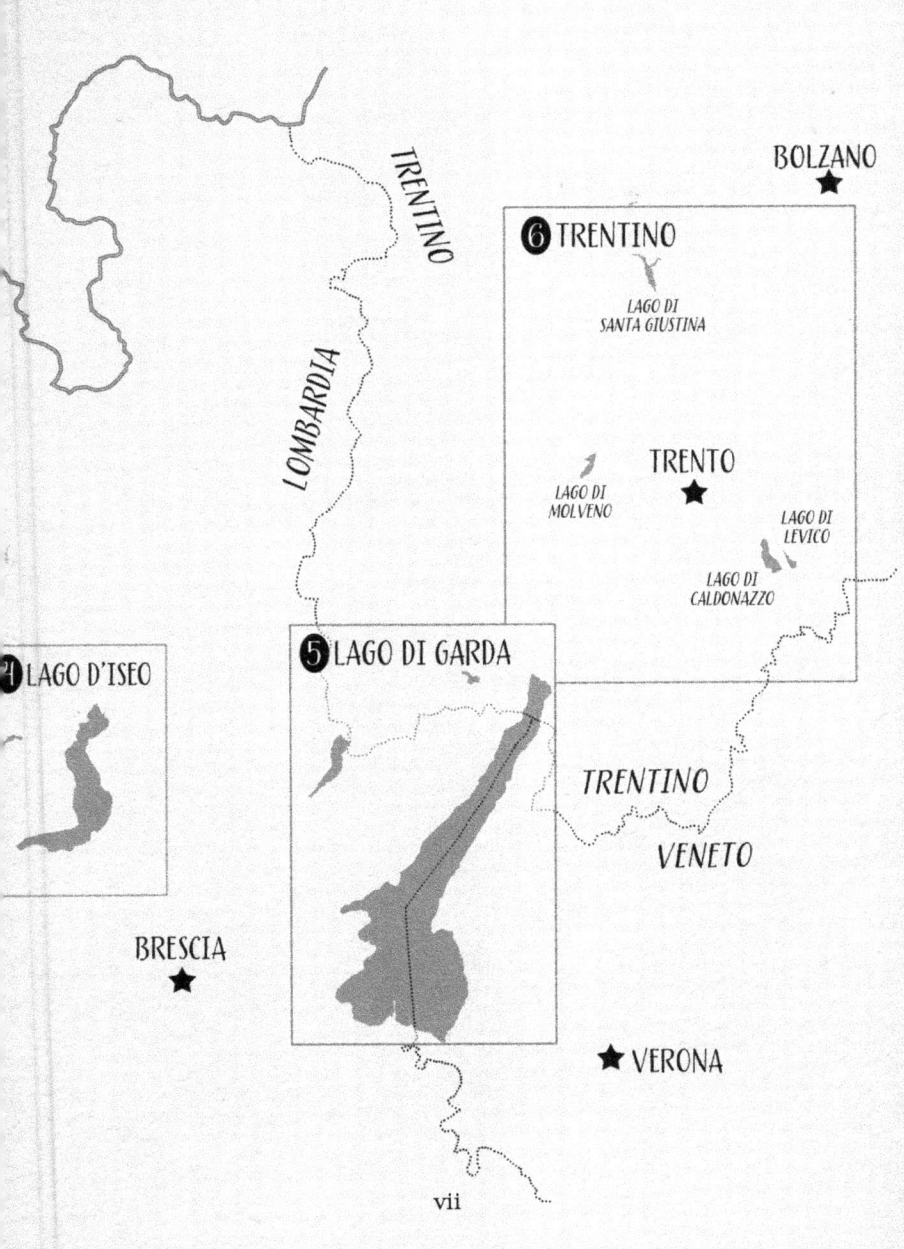

OUR GOALS

Wherever we travel, our goals are always the same:

★ Adapting to the culture and interacting with the locals;

★ Experiencing life beyond what one finds as a typical tourist;

★ Slowing down and allowing ourselves time to take in everything around us;

★ Learning about the food, culture and history of the area; and

★ Avoiding tourist crowds whenever possible.

ABOUT THIS BOOK

The Alpine Lakes regions of northern Italy are natural attractions for tourists—everyone loves the idea of lounging around at the waterside, enjoying a cocktail or coffee or a fantastic meal with the monumental Alps jutting out of every vista. These lakes are therefore heavily visited—especially in certain locations. Whether it's to take in the lavish beauty of the lakes or to explore the countless historical sites or the chance to catch a glimpse of George Clooney in his bathing suit on a yacht, people are drawn to these places in droves. We've done a great deal of exploring here ourselves; we've sought out a good many places that avoid the tourist hot-spots in favor of locations that are gorgeous, peaceful, authentic, unique, and—in the case of the food—delicious. Following along with us through these lakes, you'll discover architecture and artwork spanning millennia; you'll explore historical sights from Roman times through medieval and Renaissance cultures; you'll immerse yourself in the culture; and you'll eat more fish than you can count.

In short, this is a guidebook for those who wish to get off the beaten track and have an immersive and authentic small-town experience. We delve deeply into the countryside, down the little roads.

We find out-of-the-way sights, great local restaurants, and unique lodging, many of which have little or no presence on the internet or in other guidebooks.

Planning a Trip to Italy's Lakes

The best way to explore Italy's lakes is by car. This book contains six driving adventures, covering the different and diverse regions from Piemonte in the west, through Lombardia in the center and Trentino to the north, over to the Veneto in the east. A seventh chapter deals with a couple of choice locations near the Milan-Malpensa airport.

We have created each "route" to be quite loose, designed to allow you to go at your own pace, rather than giving specific day-by-day direction. We advise to allow yourself anywhere from a couple of days to a week for each one, and even more time if you have it. Moreover, some of them will easily overlap with one another, and the southern parts of some of the routes can be combined with routes from our other guidebook, *Emilia-Romagna: A Personal Guide to Little-known Places Foodies Will Love*. **This book is not meant to be a comprehensive, all-inclusive guide.** Rather, it is a collection of memorable places that we've found over our years of traveling in the lakes. While we provide rough maps in this book, you'll still want to have a good road map of the region.

When planning a trip to Italy, the typical tendency is to cover as much ground as possible and see the most "important" sights:

"Leaning Tower—check. Roman Forum—check. Rialto Bridge—check. Statue of David—check. Hurry—we're only halfway through the list and we only have a couple of days left!"

We encourage you to throw out that checklist, as it is the same list as that of thousands of other tourists. An overly-packed schedule is a harsh mistress; if you want a minute-by-minute to-do list, you could have stayed at work. If you want an authentic experience, you need to allow yourself time to have one: Time to have a long lunch, to converse with locals, to explore a side street or an unexpected sight, to relax and breathe.

As itinerary planners, we have talked many clients out of some of the "must-see" destinations in favor of little-known places. They always return rested, fulfilled, and carrying life-long memories of their experiences.

The excursions in this book will guide you through some of the most beautiful countryside, take you to some fascinating locations, and lead you to some of the most delicious food and drink experiences you'll ever find.

Our way of traveling is different

As professional classical musicians, Zeneba was the Artistic Director and Matt was the Operations Manager of the Grammy-nominated ALIAS Chamber Ensemble. We put a great deal of time and thought into creating interesting and diverse programs for concerts. By the time we founded the group, we had already performed much of the standard and often-heard music by famous composers. We decided to try something more adventurous. As a result the ensemble made a name for itself for commissioning new music, finding and performing great but unusual pieces by little-known composers, and occasionally offering lesser-known works by the great masters. The result became an eclectic concert experience that has something for everyone, while introducing audiences to new ways of listening to music.

When we started traveling to Europe, we applied the same general idea to our travel philosophy: After checking off the obligatory visits to the A-list locations (the Roman Colosseum, the Tower of London, Venice, Stonehenge, and the like), we started looking for more authentic, out-of-the-way experiences. We found them down the little roads of Europe—the small towns, the remote abbeys and castles, the ruins of Roman outposts, and of course the Grandma's-kitchen cuisine. This was a more immersive experience, visiting places without tourists but rich with culture, art, architecture, history, and food.

Overwhelmed by the prospect of planning an Italy trip? Little Roads Europe offers travel consulting and itinerary building services. We've created the trip of a lifetime for many happy clients.

Find out more at
www.LittleRoadsEurope.com/reserve

Driving in the Lakes Regions

In the appendix we offer a few basic tips on driving in Italy. In this mountainous Alpine region, though, a few points specific to the terrain are worth noting.

• The roads here traverse huge mountains as well as dozens of lakes. As a result, many of the routes travel right through long swaths of solid rock. These marvels of engineering range from short little passages carved into a cliff, to miles-long stretches of artificially-lit tunnels. Each tunnel (*galleria*) is preceded with a sign naming it and indicating its length in meters (or kilometers), so you know how long you have to keep your claustrophobia in check—and your headlights on.

• Most of the lakes are circled by both a lakeside road and a bypass highway. Be sure to note on your road maps (or GPS mapping device) which one you're on and where you're headed—or you may drive right past your destination and have to backtrack considerably. Sometimes the main highway is right on the water, other times it's a couple of blocks up the hill—and sometimes it's a couple hundred meters under solid rock.

- From November through April, snow chains or snow tires are required when driving in Italy. We discuss this at greater length in the appendices. (The fact that we've never actually needed them doesn't mitigate the legal mandate.)

Exploring the Lakes by Boat

On each of the larger lakes—Garda, Maggiore, Como, Iseo—a boat service operates, criss-crossing between the major towns and a few of the minor ones. It works just like a bus service—check their schedules, which are listed on a board at every

boat stop. You can also grab a paper one to carry with you. Tickets are sold at a *biglietteria* by the dock, or sometimes at a nearby bar; most of the boats are now equipped to sell tickets on board as well. These boats are often the easiest way to cover a lot of ground when visiting the lakes, good for easy transportation between locations, or even simply for a scenic ride. Just be aware of the schedules—if you miss the last boat off the island or to the other side of the lake, you may be in for an expensive cab ride, an irritating bus trip, an expensive overnight stay, or a really long swim!

Food of the Northern Lakes

Food typical in these regions include:

Polenta in many forms

Riso (rice) - *risotto* and other dishes

Gorgonzola - this is the home of the well-known, strong cheese

Bresaola - a dried, salted meat, usually beef but sometimes pork (or horsemeat!)

Carne di cavallo - horsemeat—look for words like *cavallo* or *equine*; sometimes served as *sfilacci* (strips of meat) or *spezzatino*, stewed or roasted pieces, sometimes on a *spieda* (skewer).

Pesci - fish: see next page.

Vino

We've rarely had a bad glass of wine anywhere in the north, at any price. The *vino della casa* in a restaurant is not bottom-of-the-barrel, but rather a variety selected with care for quality and value. That said, here are just a few of the many wines to watch out for, for which these regions are particularly known:

- Barbaresco in the west (Piemonte), made from nebbiolo grapes

- Franciacorta in the center, especially the sparkling whites (Lombardia)

- Teroldego in the northeast (Trentino)

- White Soave and red Valpolicella in the east (Veneto)

Pesci

***Pesci di laghi* (lake fish)** Many types of *pesce*—fish—live in Italy's lakes. Here are a few of the common

words you'll find on menus in these areas:

Alici, acciughe - anchovies, extremely salty

Alborella - bleaks—little white fish, often fried whole

Missoltini (*sarda, agone*) - splayed, salted and dried on racks—later flattened and preserved in oil

Persico (perch), *tinca* (tench), *lavarello, coregone* (common whitefish)—similar sized, white and flaky when cooked

Salmerino (Arctic char), *trota* (trout), *salmone* (salmon)—pink when cooked, oilier and more "fishy"

Luccio (pike) - *spigola, branzino* (bass)—larger, more oily fish, sometimes served encrusted with salt, carved up tableside by the *cameriere*.

Anguilla (eel)

Gamberi, gamberone, gamberetti, scampi (shrimp/prawns/crayfish) - "gamberi" is sometimes used in a general sense to refer to any of these shellfish. You may also see *cicale di mare*—

literally, "cicada of the sea"—a rare shrimp-like critter.

* Bonus food vocabulary tip *

Avoid confusion and embarrassment at seafood restaurants and also at juice bars, with the following little nugget of wisdom:

Pesce (plural: *pesci*) is "fish", pronounced "PESH-ay" and "PESH-ee".

Pesche is "peaches", pronounced "PESS-kay". Note the difference.

Buon appetito!

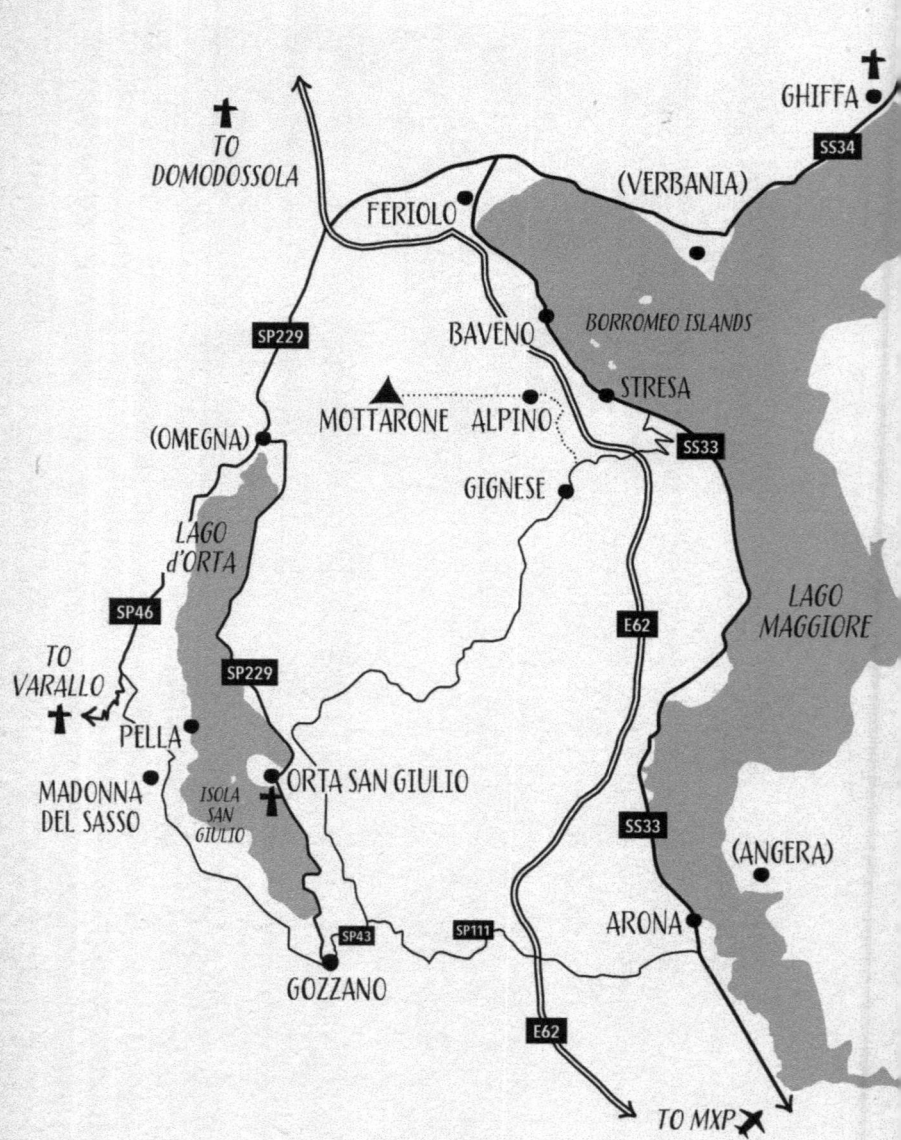

ROUTE #1

Lago d'Orta and West Lago Maggiore

Just a short drive northwest of the Milan-Malpensa airport takes us to the foot of the Alpine mountains—this is the top of the Piemonte region, a name literally meaning "foothills". The white peaks of the Alps are visible in the distance, and two lakes occupy this area—one small, and the other so large that Italy itself doesn't contain it.

The westernmost of Italy's chain of Alpine lakes is Lago d'Orta. Its main town is Orta San Giulio, which sits on a peninsula jutting out into the east side of the lake. This is a bustling but adorable little village, with a large central *piazza* lined with shops and cafes directly on the lake. An elevated town hall building, the Palazzo della Comunità, provides shade and displays centuries-old frescoes.

It's easy to dine with a view here. Right on the lake sits **Ristorante Venus**, an upscale restaurant known locally for its house-made gelato, available for take-away. Next door, Leon d'Oro also has a waterside restaurant, and will serve up fresh local fish prepared right in front of you.

For a more casual and authentic experience, find the tiny family-run **Ristorante Edera**, tucked away just off the main square. The family presents traditional, local fare. Reservations are strongly recommended, because seating is limited. You'll

feel like you're a guest in the proprietors' home dining room.

A five-minute drive out of town, past the train station, is the **Agriturismo Cucchiaio di Legno**, our favorite place to eat in this area. On the way, you will pass through the village of Miasino. Take a few minutes to walk or drive through this village to see the extensive and creative murals on the walls—it's like a free open-air art museum.

Cucchiaio di Legno has no menus. Instead, each day there is a fixed multi-course meal. Everything is locally sourced, and much of what you'll eat is from the agriturismo's own farm. Though the food is of the highest quality, the atmosphere is friendly and relaxed. You will be offered second helpings for each course, and you'll be sorely tempted to indulge, as each course is incredible. But pace yourself! Don't be a hero.

One of our favorite shops is a block from the main square, tucked away on a side street. It's easy to miss, but **Idea Dolce** is a charming chocolate shop and cafe. Imaginative and artful confections line the shelves here. Grab an espresso and indulge in a couple of chocolate tastings, or get something to take home with you—if the weather isn't chocolate-meltingly hot!

Several lodgings here offer comfortable accommodations, including the **Hotel Leon d'Oro**, which offers rooms facing the water. Visitors who want something a little quieter (and less expensive) can book a room at its sister property, **La Contrada dei Monti**, a couple of blocks away up one of the little residential side streets. Up the hill on the outskirts of the town is **Hotel La Bussola**, whose proprietor speaks five languages and runs a more standard hotel operation, including a pool and balcony rooms that breathtakingly overlook the town and the lake. It's quite an experience to sit and look at the lake and listen to the hourly church bells ringing from all over the town.

For a more "live like the locals" option, book yourself at **B&B Al Dom**. The gregarious and helpful host, Massimo, will meet you on the edge of town, help you find parking, and drive you into the little *centro*, where the adorable rooms are in a beautiful historic building by the water. Some of the rooms have balconies overlooking the little lane below and the lake. Guests have access to a shady lawn by the lake, perfect for an afternoon snack and a cocktail. There's even a ladder into the lake so you can swim in the cool Orta waters.

The San Giulio peninsula is essentially one big hill, and the bulk of it is covered by the **Sacro Monte d'Orta**. This UNESCO site is several wooded acres lined with a series of 17th-century chapels ascending the hill, each with frescoes and statuary depicting a different episode of the life of San Francesco. Each chapel also displays a fresco of a hand that points the way to the next station. It's easy to see how a pilgrim might sense a spiritual presence guiding you along the path.

At the top of the hill is a church and convent dedicated to Saint Francis. The views of the lake from here are, of course, awe-inspiring, as if the centuries of historical artwork and architecture on the way up weren't enough. From the veranda, you take in some of the most beautiful vistas of the island in the lake, like an architect's model or a detail from a Renaissance painting.

> **Sacri Monti**
> The nine Sacri Monti (Sacred Mountains) in Italy are collectively listed as UNESCO World Heritage sites. They were established in the 15th and 16th centuries to become hermitage points for religious pilgrims, most of them honoring different aspects of the story of Christ and/or the Virgin Mary. The one exception is the Sacro Monte at Lago di Orta, honoring the life of Saint Francis. Each one consists of a series of between 14 and 45 chapels, each chapel containing frescoes and statuary depicting various biblical or historical episodes.

From the central *piazza* in town, grab a boat over to this island, **Isola San Giulio**. It's not the biggest island we'll visit in these lakes (that comes later, in Route #4), but it is beautiful and unique. In recent decades, this has been the home of a Benedictine convent, but its history goes back to the fifth century. The centerpiece of this cluster of houses and religious buildings is an ornate 12th-century Romanesque basilica dedicated to Saint Julius of Novara, some of whose relics (that is, his preserved body parts) are purportedly housed inside. Though most of the island is private property of the convent, it is ringed by a walkway called the *Via di Silenzio*, the Way of Silence. Every few dozen steps, a sign offers some deep wisdom (e.g., "In the silence you meet the Master," "Listen to the water, the wind, your steps…") in four languages. Another

more directly elucidating sign directs visitors to the island's one small restaurant, which provides refreshment on yet another gorgeous lakeside patio.

Driving south on the SP229 from Orta San Giulio, clockwise around the lake, you'll come to a few notable sites. Just to the south is *Spiaggia Miami*—yes, Miami Beach. We mention this only because it's the point at which you should look for the side road that leads to the trailhead for the towering Castello di Buccione. The 13th-century castle's square watchtower looms over the lake, and is visible for miles.

At the south end of the lake is the Lido di Gozzano, another beach area. The town of Gozzano itself is a bit to the south. Hidden in the old *centro* of this small but sprawling town is **Pasticceria Mazzetti**, a lovely, traditional family bakery that has been in business for nearly 140 years. The recipes are old, but the goodies are fresh every day.

Heading north on the west side of the lake (on SP46), side roads will lead down to the little villages on the water's edge. One to watch for is **Pella**, a

cute lakeside town with an excellent eatery, the **Gelateria Antica Torre**. This shop serves not just artisanal gelato (with fun flavors such as kiwi-ginger-green apple or lavender) but also made-to-order crepes, both sweet and savory. Grab a snack, sit on a bench, and while away some time looking across the lake at Isola San Giulio. Down the street, a boat service connects Pella to the island and to Orta San Giulio.

If you have time, you can catch a little "train" from Pella that will take you up the craggy granite cliff above, where you can visit the **Santuario della Madonna del Sasso**. (This site is also accessible by car.) After centuries as a source for construction materials, this cliff became the building site of a chapel in the 16th century. Two centuries later, a baroque church and tower were built in its place and dedicated to the Madonna of the Rock.

This church is perched right at the point of the granite outcropping. Avid *Lord of the Rings* fans might be reminded of the pinnacle of Minas Tirith, though we heartily discourage both self-immolation and running off the edge of the cliff!

Farther north, the serpentine SP78 road leads west away from the lake to the town of **Varallo**, above which another Sacro Monte sits. Known as *Piccolo Gerusalemme* ("Little Jerusalem") this is the oldest of the *Sacri Monti* sites, built in the late 15th century. It does seem like a city, and not a small one. Most such sites have between 14 and 24 chapels, but *Piccolo Gerusalemme* comprises nearly four dozen chapels and churches clustered together on a hill high above the convergence of two rivers.

Returning to Lake Orta, continue north to the town of Omegna, the largest town on the lake, and then to Gravellona Toce, which is named for the Fiume Toce, the river that feeds the much bigger lake we're about to visit. Following this river north (on the SS33) leads to Domodossola and another Sacro Monte site.

But this is a book about lakes, after all, so instead let's take the SS34 from Gravellona east to Lago Maggiore, Italy's second-largest lake. You'll pass through the sprawl of Verbania and come to the unassuming little village of Ghiffa. Turn on the cobbly road that leads up to the **Sacro Monte di Ghiffa**, a much smaller Sacro Monte than the others, but still a beautiful site.

This one also enjoys a stunning overlook of this huge lake and its surrounding mountains, and it has a porticoed walkway with a *Via Crucis*—frescoes depicting the life of Jesus in the Stations of the Cross. It's worth the drive to see this Sacro Monte just to take in the views of the lake far below.

If you drive much farther north on Lago Maggiore's coast road, you'll soon come to the border of Switzerland. To cross, you'll need to go through border control and purchase a Swiss highway vignette for your car—it's about 40 euros. The lake extends well into Swiss territory, up to the city of Locarno at the very north end of the lake.

Since visiting Switzerland would force us to reconsider the title of this book, we suggest instead descending from the Ghiffa holy site back down to the lake and heading south. Don't worry about missing out—there is plenty to explore around the Italian portion of the Lago Maggiore! This side of the lake is quite developed, with plenty of hotels, campgrounds, boating centers, and other tourist accommodations. What we describe herein are the places we have discovered that either keep you clear of the crowds or that we think are worth braving the bustle.

You'll come to the town of **Feriolo** shortly after crossing the Toce River where it enters the lake. In the center of town, right along the main SS33 route, is **Hotel Ristorante Serenella**. Though it's set back from the lake by a block or two, it offers a charming and affordable lodging option. From here, a stroll of two minutes brings you to

Route #1 Lago d'Orta and West Lago Maggiore

Feriolo's lakeside pedestrian zone and its little beach. The restaurant at Serenella is excellent as well, if you wish to keep away from the beach scene. The hotel and restaurant are a flowerful, peaceful haven—a little private oasis.

Further south on the SS33 is one of our favorite towns on Lago Maggiore, **Baveno**. The cobbled streets of its *centro* and its ancient porticoed church *piazza* (another *Via Crucis*) are just a few of its charms. Most of all, we love staying at **B&B La Sorgente**. Just a short walk south of town, this lodging has beautiful rooms with balconies overlooking

the lake—it's directly across from Isola Pescatori. The owners, Francesca (another multilingual host) and Riccardo, make guests feel right at home with exceptionally delicious breakfast goodies and a wealth of information and assistance. The rooms are quite affordable, especially when you factor in the large private balconies and the breakfast terrace, all of which boast unobstructed views of the lake.

The Borromeo family

The Borromeo family was one of the richest and most influential families in Italy since the 14th century. Their range of power spread from Milan to the Lago Maggiore area. Comparable to the Medici family of Tuscany—in fact the two families were connected by marriage in the 16th century—the Borromeo family tree included cardinals and counts, bankers and bishops, and all manner of powerful political personae. They left their mark in the region with dozens of castles and palaces—including the several islands on Lago Maggiore—and the aristocratic family still owns most of these properties today.

Baveno is a good place from which to explore the **Borromeo Islands** on the lake. You can buy *biglietti* (tickets) for the boat passage and entry to any or all three of the islands at the Navigazione Lago Maggiore ticket office. Be sure to ask for the ticket *andate e ritorno*—"going and returning," a.k.a. round-trip.

Isola Madre, the largest and the farthest island from the shore, is a woodsy garden paradise surrounding one of the old Borromeo family's smaller mansions. Footpaths wander among hundreds of species of flora, ranging from alpine plants to tropical flowers. Fantastical birds with incredible plumage—white peacocks are just the least of them!—meander the grounds freely. Being there feels like strolling through the mythical Garden of Paradise.

Isola Bella, close to the western shore of the lake, holds the incredible Palazzo Borromeo. This extravagant 17th-century palace is flanked by meticulously designed formal Italianate gardens (or, as they call them here in Italy, just "gardens"), stacked up on the island's hill like a giant wedding cake.

Isola Pescatori—literally and historically the fishermen's island—is the only residential island of the three. Its single church, the 11th-century Chiesa di San Vittore, contains a Madonna statue that resides in a glass hutch in one of the side altars. (She comes out for the high-summer festival of Ferragosto, when she is paraded around the town while illuminated boats circle the island.) There are several restaurants on this island, including an excellent pizzeria, **La Rondine**, with a patio on the water, naturally; and the imaginatively-named **Ristorante Italia**, which serves delicious dishes using the fish from the lake.

The island also has several shops featuring jewelry and ceramics made by local artisans.

The next town south on the lake road is **Stresa**, a large hub of tourist activity. The lakefront in the town is one splendid, palatial hotel after another, and its *centro* comprises block after block of shops, bars, and restaurants. While it is busy, we do love to stop here for a couple of choice establishments. **La Cambusa** is a cute little shop a block from the lakeside road. Here you'll find all manner of *liquori* and wines from the area and beyond, and a highly knowledgeable proprietor who can guide you to an excellent selection.

(Our favorite is a locally made *amaretto*, the only *amaretto* crafted from real almonds rather than extracts or flavorings.) A short stroll down a little side street brings you to the door of **Ristorante Il Vicoletto** (the name literally means "little alley"). This adorable restaurant offers expertly prepared and authentic local cuisine, away from the buzz of the tourists a few blocks away.

From Stresa, take the *funivia* (funicular or cable-car) up to the top of the mountain that separates Lake Orta from Maggiore. If you hop off at the "Alpino" stop, walk down the road a few minutes to the **Giardino Botanico Alpina**, a painstakingly maintained 100-year-old flowerful garden overlooking Maggiore. Or continue on the *funivia* to its final stop, the peak of **Mottarone**, for Olympian views of both lakes.

Some active travelers avail themselves of the system of hiking trails up to Mottarone from either Stresa or Baveno. It's also possible to take the *funivia* up and then walk down. Those who prefer the challenge of driving narrow, twisty roads over that of excessive walking on mountains can reach these peaks by car from Stresa. If you do this, you'll probably pass through the village of **Gignese**. Here you can eat at **Osteria delle 3 V**, named for the three siblings who run it, Vittorio, Veronica, and Virginia. The restaurant's interior is gorgeous, with a wealth of quaint copper pans

hanging from the ceiling. The specialty here is polenta in various forms, all of them deliciously filling. Before or after lunch, take a quick stroll through the quirky and historic **Museo dell'Ombrello** (Umbrella Museum). One of the town's founding fathers was an 18th-century umbrella baron—yes, that was actually a thing—and the industry was important to civic development here.

Gignese also has a little *piazza* right on the main road through town, where the locals gather for their daily newspapers, coffees, and cocktails. Watch out for servers crossing the street from the bar to serve their clientele! This street is also the highway that snakes its way across the mountains between Stresa and Orta San Giulio.

Returning back down the mountain to the lake, one more town captures our attention: **Arona**, near the south end of the lake. The town itself is large and is surrounded by modern sprawl on its outskirts, but the *centro* has a big, picturesque town *piazza* on the lake. From here you will be able to get the best view of the castle at Angera, across the lake. On days when the water is calm, the castle is reflected on the blue waters like a perfect mirror. At the edge of town is the **Parco della Rocca Borromea**, a wooded park surrounding the ruins of a Borromeo family castle. From here, the Borromeo rulers could look down imperiously at the town below and the lake beyond.

A short drive north of Arona and up the hill brings you to the **Colosso di San Carlo**. Across the street from this 115-foot statue is the Church of San Carlo (for the devout) and the Ristorante Bar San Carlo (for the thirsty). In 1624 Cardinal Federico Borromeo, the Archbishop of Milan, commissioned a colossus to depict his ancestor

Route #1   Lago d'Orta and West Lago Maggiore

San Carlo, another cardinal and archbishop. Towering at the top of the hill above Arona (Carlo was born in Arona's now-ruined castle), the bronze statue was completed in 1698. (It later became a model for the construction of the Statue of Liberty.) Visitors can climb up inside the colossus and peer out of Carlo's eyes, looking out to the eastern side of Maggiore—which is, coincidentally, where our next chapter leads us.

WHERE TO EAT

Orta San Giulio

Ristorante Venus
Modern Italian cuisine in a beautiful restaurant right on the lake. Large outdoor seating area in summer. In winter, window tables have the best views of Isola San Giulio. Open for lunch and dinner. Closed Mondays.
> http://www.venusorta.it

Agriturismo Cucchiaio di Legno
Our favorite place to eat in this itinerary. Multi-course meals with a fixed menu that changes daily and seasonally. Rooms here also, for a more rural stay. Open for dinner Thursday-Sunday, Saturday and Sunday also lunch. Reservations required. 30€/pp, not including wine.
> http://www.ilcucchiaiodilegno.com/

Ristorante San Giulio (Isola San Giulio)
The only restaurant on Orta's only island, a peaceful and gorgeous place to have a quiet lunch. Open for lunch six days a week, dinner also Thursday-Saturday. Closed Tuesdays. Closed during the winter months, so be sure to call ahead if traveling in off-season.
> https://www.ristorantesangiulio.com/

Pella

Gelateria Antica Torre

Artisan gelato maker right by the water. All *gelati* made in-house, specializing in unusual and interesting flavor combinations. Sweet or savory crepes here, hand-made to order. A great, quick and affordable lunch spot. Open every day from 10am-11pm.

http://gelateriaanticatorre.com/

Stresa

Ristorante Il Vicoletto

Tucked away on a small side street, a welcome oasis of high-end cuisine among a plethora of restaurants catering to tourists. Reservations recommended. Open for lunch and dinner Friday-Wednesday. Closed Thursday.

http://gelateriaanticatorre.com/

Gignese

Osteria Tre V

Friendly, family-run place in a residential neighborhood. Like a little museum, its walls adorned with photos and mementos of local people and history. Polenta is the specialty here. Closed Monday all day and Tuesday dinner; otherwise open for lunch and dinner. In July and August, no closing days.

http://www.osteriadelle3v.it/

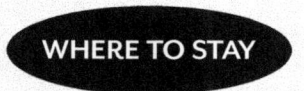

Orta San Giulio

La Contrada dei Monti
Cozy hotel on a small street right in the center of town, quite close to the public (pay) garage. A little hidden courtyard for guests to enjoy. Breakfast in the morning at sister hotel, Leon d'Oro, a few minutes walk away.

http://www.lacontradadeimonti.it/en/

Hotel La Bussola
Large hotel right next to the public parking lot, just on the edge of town. Lake-view balcony rooms, beautiful views of the lake and Isola san Giulio. Pool and free parking.

https://www.hotelbussolaorta.it/en/

B&B Al Dom
Beautiful rooms with mini fridges, some with small balconies. The real luxury of this place is its private garden right on the lake, with tall shade trees and plenty of beautiful places to sit or to dry off after a dip in the lake. A private courtyard in the B&B interior for guests to enjoy.

https://aldom57.com/

Feriolo

Hotel Ristorante Serenella
A beautiful little hotel restaurant set away from the busy street, just a two-minute walk to the lakefront. Free parking on site. Restaurant has some of the best food in the area.

http://www.hotelserenella.net/en

Baveno

B&B La Sorgente

Among many lodging options on Maggiore, this one holds a special place in our hearts. Unbeatable balcony views—we have eaten many picnic dinners here overlooking the lake. Owner Francesca makes a delicious breakfast in a country not known for its breakfasts. She makes visitors feel welcome immediately. A treasure.

http://lasorgente.biz/en/

Isola dei Pescatori

Ristorante Italia

A hotel as well as a restaurant. We love to stay overnight on this little island. Romantic and nearly deserted once the day-trippers go home in the evening. One room with a large balcony, the perfect place to spend the afternoon hours while the crowds are heavy in high season.

http://www.ristoranteitalia-isolapescatori.it/

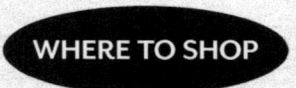

Orta San Giulio

Idea Dolce

A little chocolate shop and cafe tucked away down a small alley, just off the main square. Offers savory lunches, but we prefer to stop for a cappuccino and to try a few handmade chocolates or pastries. Hours vary and they have no website. Via Olina, 7, 28016 Orta San Giulio

Gozzano

Pasticceria Mazzetti
We love this little bakery, which has been in the same family for nearly 140 years. Open Tuesday-Saturday 8:30-12:30 and 2:30 - 7:30, Sunday 8am-6:30. Closed Monday.
https://www.pasticceriamazzetti.com/

Stresa

Enoteca La Cambusa
More than once, we've driven well out of our way to shop here. The Bolla family, who own this shop, are knowledgeable and helpful. They stock the only *amaretto* (Amaretto di Stresa) made from real almonds—you can absolutely taste the difference.
http://www.enotecalacambusastresa.com/

Alpino

Giardino Botanico Alpina
Beautiful Alpine garden, sweeping lake views. A peaceful respite, especially in high summer when the lakeside can be crowded. Open every day from 9:30-6pm, from early April to early October. 4€/pp.
http://giardinobotanicoalpinia.altervista.org/

Gignese

Umbrella Museum
A quirky and fun little museum. While it focuses on umbrellas and their importance in the culture, it also has quite a bit of local history and artifacts. Open Monday - Saturday 10-12 and 3-6. Closed Sunday. 2.50€/pp.
http://www.gignese.it/museo/

Arona

Colosso di San Carlo
For two centuries, this was the tallest statue in the world. It remains among the world's largest to this day. Climb inside to literally see the lake through the Colosso's eyes. Opening times vary by season, check here:
https://www.statuasancarlo.it/

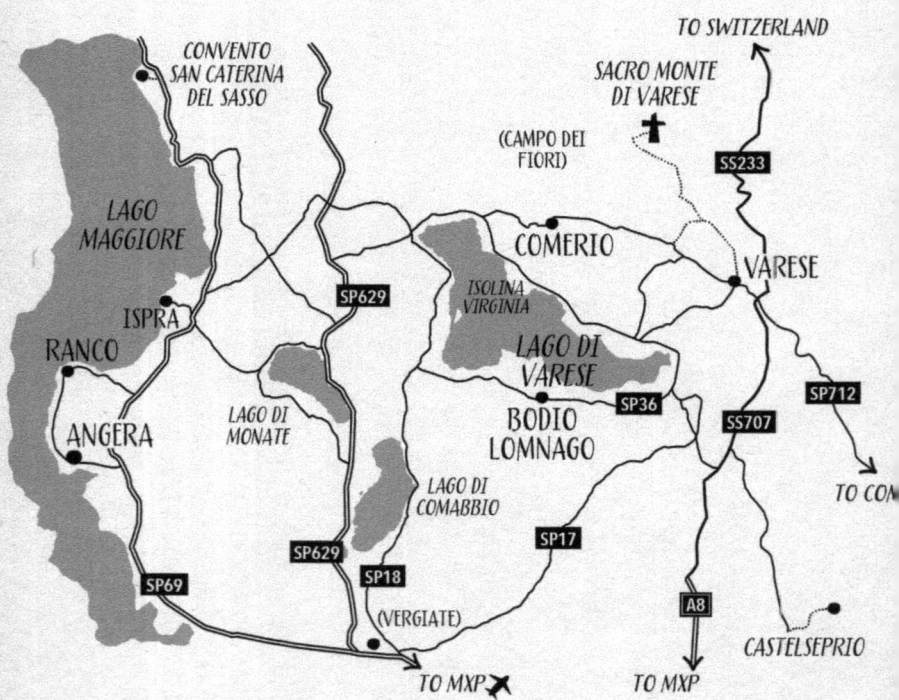

ROUTE #2

East Lago Maggiore and Lago di Varese

The terrain from the southeast side of Lago Maggiore to Lago di Varese is generally flatter than in the west. The mountains loom not far away, though, and the hills hold their secrets and their treasures.

The line dividing the Piemonte region from Lombardia goes straight down Lago Maggiore. In addition to fish dishes from the lakes, one of the most famous foodstuffs of the Lombard region is *gorgonzola*, having originated in the town of the same name. Fans of that particular stinky cheese should look for it on menus here.

It's a short passenger ferry ride from Arona to Angera, straight across the southern foot of Lago Maggiore. If you're traveling by car (as we always are), it's about a half-hour drive around the south end of the lake. You'll cross the Ticino, the river that flows from the Swiss Alps into Lago Maggiore and then exits the lake here to flow south into the

Route #2 East Lago Maggiore and Lago di Varese

Po River in Emilia-Romagna. Take the Via Angera highway to the small town of **Angera**. Here, a public park runs along a good length of the lakeside—a long stretch of tree-lined green space where you can picnic, walk the dog, watch the shore birds and boaters, have a sandwich and coffee at a lakeside cafe, and take in the view of Arona and the Colosso di San Carlo across the lake. At the northern end of the park is where the Navigazione Lago Maggiore boats set out for other points on the lake.

Angera has many hotels and restaurants, including the Albergo Pavone, which is set off down a little street a block from the main strip. Attached to the hotel is the **Ristorante Vecchia Angera** restaurant, where one of the dishes is a pasta (or risotto) prepared at your table *in forma*: The

cameriere stirs hot pasta around in a large, hollowed-out wheel of *parmigiano-reggiano* cheese. The heat melts the cheese enough to create a creamy coating on the pasta, making an entertaining as well as delicious experience.

Perched on a cliff above the town is the castle that's visible from much of the western side of the lake, the imposing **Rocca di Angera**. For a change, this 13th-century castle *wasn't* originally built by the wealthy Borromeos -but they did buy it two centuries later and improved upon it over subsequent centuries. Huge rooms filled with centuries of artwork give visitors a feel for the sweep of

> **Gorgonzola and DOC**
>
> Many foods in Italy are labeled with acronyms. These are marks of quality foods produced to exacting standards, like DOC or DOCG (*Denominazione di Origine Controllata e Garantita*) for wine; or IGP (*Indicazione Geografica Protetta*) for various foodstuffs specific to certain geographic regions. Gorgonzola cheese, which originated in Piemonte and Lombardia, has a DOP (*Denominazione di Origine Protetta*) status: The standards are high, maintained by various food consortiums nationwide. The classification speaks to the processes of production and sources of ingredients, which are highly specific.

history the castle has witnessed. Climb to the top of the tower for spectacular views over the town and the lake. A large and beautiful Italian garden flanks the castle at the edge of the cliff.

The castle also hosts a unique attraction: The **Museo della Bambola**, or "Doll Museum." A dozen rooms are dedicated to displays of dolls and

toys from several centuries and continents. A stroll through these rooms is interesting, but can also be disquieting: Some of the doll faces are a little creepy, and a few are positively homicidal. We advise making sure you get through this section of the castle well before the doors are locked at night.

If Angera is too busy for your taste, drive just a bit farther north to the little village of **Ranco**. Here the flowerful **Hotel Ristorante Belvedere** offers airy rooms that come with fluffy robes and slippers. The nicest rooms have balconies with gorgeous views of the lake. The best views from the hotel are to be found on the covered patio on the ground floor, which in warmer months holds tables for the hotel's excellent restaurant. Belvedere means "beautiful view," and this establishment is certainly appropriately named. Below the hotel on the water is another town park, suitable for picnicking, walking, or lounging at the lakeside bar.

Farther north, up the eastern edge of the lake, the SP69 road diverts away from the water until you pass through Arolo and reach the monastery of **Santa Caterina del Sasso**. This is a fascinating but heavily visited site, a series of religious structures dating as far back as the 12th century. These churches and chapels and cloisters cling to the rocky cliffs (*sasso* means "rock" or "stone") and come right up to the water's edge. We recommend visiting this site by boat (the public ferry service stops here), as the best views of this monastery are from the water.

From here, the SP69 runs closer to the lake's edge, making for a nicer drive up to the remaining towns before reaching Switzerland. (See Route 1 regarding crossing the Swiss border by car.) To avoid running afoul of the Swiss authorities, we turn west now towards **Lago di Varese**. Smaller even than Lake Orta, Varese is popular for its circumferential running/biking path, and for watersports such as rowing. In its vicinity there are several sites that are well worth visiting.

At the west end of the lake there is a tiny island just off the shore, **Isolino Virginia**. You can reach it from the boat station at a little park in the town of Biandronno. This island is a UNESCO location, the site of a Neolithic-era pile-dwelling community. Ancient builders (thousands of years B.C.) drove logs straight down into the mud and used these stilts as the foundation of their buildings. Archaeologists have determined that this is the oldest-known settlement in the Italian pre-alpine region. Today a museum and a restaurant sit on this otherwise unspoiled piece of historical real estate.

Continuing to the south edge of the lake, we come to the village of Bodio Lomnago. The boutique hotel **Equirelais** sits next to an equestrian school—hence the name. Its patio and lawn enjoy sweeping views of the lake and the stables next door. Only one room (a suite) has a lake view, but all the rooms are spacious and immaculate. The restaurant downstairs offers limited food options but a full bar. For a more upscale experience, the nearby hotel **Villa Baroni** has balcony rooms and also impeccable food, sourced locally and presented exquisitely.

On the north side of the lake, two locations bear mentioning. In the town of Comerio, the **Parco di Villa Tatti Tallacchini** is a large-scale terraced Italian garden. Formerly part of the villa property above it, the broad green space is now a free public park. Here, mothers push strollers and artists sit and draw amidst centuries-old garden landscaping. A balcony at one end looks out over the lake, a small taste of what the view from the villa itself must be. The walls surrounding a large fountain are inset with ornate sculpture, including several friezes of mythological figures in bas-relief. One depicts the tale of Arion, a Greek musician who was kidnapped by pirates and rescued by dolphins. This park is an unusual example of the wealthy ceding a sizeable portion of their precious land for the public good.

Just a couple of minutes away is another kind of oddity, The **Pub Locanda dello Hobbit**. The proprietors here are avid fans of J.R.R. Tolkien's beloved characters, and indeed of anything in the realm of medieval fantasy. A simple food list (with sandwiches and pizzas named for characters from Middle Earth) is complemented by a room full of all the trappings of a British pub—a dark wood bar, old swords and armor, and an excellent array of draft beers. Don't spend too much time trying to figure out what unicorns or menorahs have to do with hobbits, just enjoy your beer. We don't consider this a "foodie" stop, but visiting this place makes for a fun and unexpected journey.

Work your way east and up the Campo dei Fiori, toward the medieval hilltop town of **Santa Maria del Monte**, which is the pinnacle of the **Sacro Monte di Varese**. Fourteen chapels from the early 17th century stand along a winding footpath that begins about a mile down the hill and ends at the town's incredible Santuario. Make sure you have plenty of time to explore this huge and ornate church, including its interior chapels. The town also has a couple of museums, a monastery, and a maze of pedestrian streets that twist and turn back on each other. As the town is

built on a mountain, its streets are steep. But if you crave more arduous exercise, there are hiking trails from the north edge of town that lead into the woods and up to the Campo dei Fiori peak.

If you feel your devotion is best shown in more of a state of repose, stay at the beautiful **Hotel Ristorante Colonne** on the edge of the town. Its staff is friendly, its rooms have balconies, and its restaurant offers Michelin-star dining. Up the street a bit is the **Hotel Al Borducan**, with the same views and the added benefit of its proprietary *liquore*, the smooth, tasty and locally famous Elixir di Borducan. Just a few steps away, you'll find the little shop **Emporio del Sacro Monte di Varese,** which sells local food, wine, and crafts. Be sure to try the "Mustazitt," a tiny, rock-hard cookie made from a centuries-old local recipe, created by a chef to the Pope. Mustazitts are meant to be held in the mouth like a lozenge until they soften enough to be chewed. (Alternatively, you can dip them in Elixir di Borducan.)

Route #2 East Lago Maggiore and Lago di Varese

Coming back down the mountain, you'll come to the town of Varese. Historically an important hub of power and commerce, this is a big and sprawling town, with a web of confusing streets and a lot of traffic. Though Varese has many impressive churches and palaces, a charming pedestrian zone and green parks and engaging museums, we usually give it a pass in search of more placid places.

The Longobards

Before the Borromeos, there were the Longobardi. These weren't a family, but rather a tribe of people from Germania who migrated into northern Italy after the fall of the Roman Empire. They ruled the north (and indeed much of the Italian peninsula) from the 6th to the 8th century, and they were largely responsible for establishing a great many settlements and fortifications in the region. Their name eventually morphed into "Lombardi", and it was this that gave the name to the vast region of Italy from Lago Maggiore in the west to Lago di Garda far to the east.

Two such sites lie waiting about a 20-minute drive south of Varese into the countryside: The **Monastero di Torba** and the settlement of **Castelseprio**. These were two of many settlements of the powerful Longobard people, who ruled the region from the sixth to the eighth centuries. Originally a Roman outpost built as a bastion against the barbarian hordes (and we know how that worked out for the Romans), Torba was later converted to a monastic complex. This site is part of the Fondo Ambiente Italiano (FAI), an Italian historic preservation organization. Today FAI has created a historical museum here, where visitors can get a feel for life in the early Middle Ages. Just through the woods is the archaeological park at the ruins of Castelseprio. This was another Longobard settlement connected to the Torba monastery, a walled village built on Roman ruins. A huge (for its time) basilica was built here in the fifth century, which now lies in impressive ruins. Later church structures at the site are more intact, including a ninth-century church to the west of the fortifications. The whole Castelseprio settlement was destroyed in the 13th century, but this church escaped destruction due to its religious importance and its position as the Chiesa di Santa Maria Foris Portas (the last two words of which mean "outside the gates"). It's a lucky thing, too. The church's walls hold some of the earliest

Route #2 East Lago Maggiore and Lago di Varese

medieval frescoes in all of Europe, and they're largely intact.

Angera

Ristorante Vecchia Angera
Large restaurant right in the center of Angera, attached to the Hotel Albergo Pavone. Pizza also available.
> http://www.hotelpavone.it/

Bodio Lomnago

Villa Baroni
Upscale restaurant serving modern Italian fare in an elegant setting. See our listing in "Where To Stay" as well. Lunch and dinner Tuesday - Sunday, closed on Monday.
> http://www.villabaroni.it

Santa Maria del Monte

Hotel Ristorante Colonne
Treat yourself to a special meal in the mountains at this restaurant that has a Michelin star. The restaurant is the more upscale establishment, the bistro offers excellent fare in a cozier setting a little more affordably. (Also see listing in Where To Stay)
> http://www.albergocolonne.it/

Ranco

Hotel Ristorante Belvedere
Excellent food at a beautiful restaurant with expansive lake views. The west side of the lake is less crowded and so it's peaceful here even in summertime. Lunch and dinner offered in summer; off season, hours vary. Closed Wednesdays.
> https://www.hotelristorantebelvedere.it

Ranco

Hotel Ristorante Belvedere
Gorgeous rooms with mini fridges, fluffy robes, and many have balconies overlooking the lake.

https://www.hotelristorantebelvedere.it

Bodio Lomnago

Villa Baroni
Beautiful lakeside hotel with a pool above a fantastic restaurant, just 30 minutes from Milan's airport.

http://www.villabaroni.it

Equirelais
Very comfortable rooms in a new structure with a large patio and lawn space, across the street from a horse farm. There is a bar and restaurant here as well.

http://www.equirelais.it

Santa Maria del Monte

Hotel Ristorante Colonne
Beautiful hotel in an idyllic mountaintop location. Ask for one of the rooms with a balcony for beautiful views down the mountain to Lago Varese. (See listing above in Where To Eat)

http://www.albergocolonne.it/

Sacro Maria del Monte

Emporio del Sacro Monte di Varese
A small little shop stocked with local goodies and crafts. Open 10-12:30 on weekdays, and 10-4:30 on weekends.
http://www.sacromontevarese.net/it/emporio

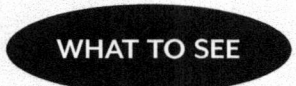

Angera

Rocca di Angera
Beautiful and extensive castle, commanding views of the lake. The Doll Museum really creeped us out but also gave us years of jokes. 9.50€/pp; combination tickets for the castle and the islands are also available.
http://www.isoleborromee.it/eng/angera.html

Leggiuno

Santa Caterina del Sasso
Catholics may want to attend Holy Mass, which is held here every Sunday at 4:30pm. It is free to enter the site, but hours vary according to season, see full details here:
http://www.santacaterinadelsasso.com/

Torba

Monastero di Torba

A valuable historic site just 30 minutes from Milan's airport. 7€ entry, reduced fees for families, students, and children. Hours vary by season; full timetables here:
https://www.fondoambiente.it/luoghi/monastero-di-torba

Gornate Olona

Castelseprio

Large archaeological park dating to the Bronze Age, also an important religious site with a museum. Free entry. The site is closed December and January, opening times vary by season and can be found here:
http://www.unescovarese.com/castelseprio

ROUTE #3

Lago di Como

The original name for this lake was not Como, but Lago di Lario, which comes from a Latin derivation. The historical prominence of the city of Como, however, led people over the centuries to refer to the lake as Lago di Como, and that name sticks to this day.

But the names of many lake towns here still include the word Lario, and the typical cuisine of the lake is called *cucina Lariana*. Lake Como is probably best known as a vacation home for various rich

Route #3 Lago di Como

and famous glitterati—Clooney, Versace, Madonna, Branson, and more—and consequently its major towns tend to be crowded with throngs of celebrity seekers as well as upscale travelers. As with all our travels, we've made an effort to explore this lake to find authentic places away from the crowds.

Como is Italy's deepest lake—well over 1300 feet deep—and the steep surrounding mountains on all sides seem to highlight this point. Lake Como is shaped like an inverted Y with two "legs" converging into a single upper segment. We start at the top of the western leg, above the town of

Ossuccio. Stretched out on the mountain here is the **Sacro Monte di Ossuccio**, a series of 14 chapels leading up to its peak and the 16th-century Santuario della Beata Vergine del Soccorso. This is probably the most challenging of the Sacri Monti sites in this book. Unless you're one of the clergy or you have a donkey, walking the steep path to the top is the only option. It's also one of the most rewarding walks, as the views are stunning. Looking down from up here, you'll see the large town of **Lenno** and a big forested hill sticking out into the lake. That's a wooded park area, at the end of which is the **Villa del Barbianello**. This villa is a now-popular tourist attraction due to its status as the filming site for many movies, including *Casino Royale* and (albeit much-obscured by CGI) *Star Wars Episode II*. Setting aside James Bond and clone attacks in favor of our interest in food, Lenno is also home to the **Oleificio Osvaldo**, a maker of a highly-regarded olive oil. Their shop sells the precious culinary commodity as is, and also offers soaps and skin creams made from it.

Continue south on the SS340 highway to the town of **Sala Comacina**. Just before the town you'll see an interesting church on your left, the

11th-century **Chiesa di San Giacomo**. It contains ancient frescoes inside and out, including on the wall facing the highway. Although this stretch of the lake is lined with touristy towns and ritzy hotels, Sala Comacina seems relatively ignored due to its driving challenges. Visitors must park just off the busy highway up the hill, and then walk down into the village. Once you do this, though, you're in a quiet little haven, with ample bars and restaurants but sparse crowds. The town has a lovely little public beach area filled with sand for kids and adults to enjoy waterside recreation.

A small fee buys you passage from the town marina across to the ancient **Isola Comacina**. A sign-posted tour takes visitors along footpaths through the island's ruins and its history. One story has it that in the sixth century, a clergyman was transporting the Holy Grail from Britain to Rome. Stopped by Longobard forces in this region, he took refuge on this tiny island. This gave rise to several religious enclaves, and today the island is home to the remains of several ancient churches and the thousand-year-old **Monastero di San Faustino**.

(At some point in the ensuing millennium, the Grail must have been relocated elsewhere.)

In any case, this island has no shortage of loaves and fishes. This is a quintessential foodie stop. The iconic **Locanda dell'Isola Comacina**, which sits on a hill facing the town, has served a fantastic and unchanging meal of traditional dishes since 1948. There's no menu; every table receives the same bountiful courses for a fixed price. The starter is a giant loaf of crusty bread (meant to be ripped by hand) with a simple tomato that's topped with olive oil, oregano, and a paper-thin lemon slice. These are meant to be eaten all together. Next, assorted cured meats accompany a variety of about a dozen fresh, pickled, roasted, and otherwise expertly prepared vegetables and beans. These vary by the season, and all are of the absolute highest quality. There is no pasta course

here. Instead, there are two meat courses. First, you receive a grilled salmon trout, presented and dished up tableside. Next is a crunchy fried chicken with a salad of perfect butter lettuce on the side. Finally, the dessert course consists of fruit and gelato, drizzled with the liqueur that's made on the island. Although the staff here are friendly and relaxed, the service is impeccable. As you enjoy your leisurely lunch, you'll observe little boats coming and going from the dock below, delivering some of the prime foodstuffs that the restaurant serves. From here you can also see the aforementioned church of San Giacomo, clutching as if for dear life on the lake's edge.

At the end of the meal, a ceremony is performed. The head of the house rings a bell to get diners' attention, then delivers a short presentation about island history. While the story is told, a huge cauldron of coffee is mixed with brandy and lit on fire, then distributed to the guests. This is a perfect example of the type of "Little Roads" place we love: authentic, traditional, relaxed, of the highest quality, but still feeling like you're eating in someone's home. The word "lunch" seems inadequate for such an epic meal. Along that line, make sure to do the walking tour of the island *before* you eat, as you'll need to be rolled home afterward.

Returning to the mainland, follow the road south. You'll pass by the little town of Argegno, whose small town *piazza* is a gathering place right on the highway. Among the shops and restaurants here is **Gelato di Zoe** - in high demand due to the boat and bus traffic, but worth the wait. A block away is a picturesque stone footbridge that crosses a little creek plunging down from the mountain above.

Still farther south is the village of Brienno. Passing through a short tunnel, you'll see a short

bit of street parking on the lake side. This is for a small complex of religious structures—a couple of chapels, a cemetery, and the 18th-century **Chiesa della Madonna dell'Immacolata**. Beneath this church complex is a tunnel that's part of World War I history: a *Galleria di Mina*, or mine tunnel. This was a defensive position that was meant to be demolished in the case of enemy advancement along this important transportation route. Fortunately, it never had to be used as such, so the above sacred site remains intact.

This stretch of highway is one from which smaller roads divert to pass through the little towns directly on the lake. At Laglio, take the smaller lake road and work your way toward Carate Urio, where a driveway leads to a little enclave where there are two stellar lodging options. The luxurious **Tiziana's Suite** provides a just-like-living-here lodging. The apartment itself is small and lovely, with two bedrooms and a little balcony. The real prize here, though,

is a few dozen steps outside, more or less straight up the side of the cliff: a small patio with a sweeping view. Tiziana herself lives downstairs and offers a breakfast on her beautiful flowery patio, complete with fresh-baked *cornetti* (croissants). Next door is **Ai Cedri**, a four-bedroom home, with light, airy rooms and a private garden. Both of these properties share beautiful views and at-your-door parking. As they are set above the road, the quiet and seclusion at either is a perfect refuge from the Como crowds. Several restaurants are within walking distance of the house. Better yet, come prepared with a few well-chosen groceries and bottles, and enjoy your own private dinner with the best view in town. Wave to the boats as they go by on the lake below. You'll be the envy of all the passers-by, even the ones on yachts!

Proceed south on the SS340 to Cernobbio. This is a town with an old *centro* that's surrounded by a large modern sprawl. It's possible to bypass much of the town on the highway, and head through to the city of Como. Although it's full of rich history and beautiful architecture, including several stunning and huge churches, Como town is, for us, dauntingly large. (And, in any case it's well-covered by countless guidebooks.) Therefore we suggest making your way around it, although that's easier said than done, as its few circumventing highways are confusingly marked at times.

Once around Como, proceed north up the SP583, on the east side of the lake's left leg, past Torno.

Missoltini

Visitors to Italy's lakes—especially Como and Iseo—will occasionally see an array of fish splayed and hanging in the sun on racks. These are *sarda* or *agoni*—a type of shad. The fish are prepared with salt for two days and then dried for a month or more, before being flattened and preserved in oil and herbs, and packed for later eating. This method of preparation and preservation dates back to the middle ages, when the fish were preserved in a wooden container called a *missolta*—from which comes the name of this dish, *missoltini*.

This part of the drive becomes more challenging, but it's lovely, with narrower roads, turns that hug the cliff face, and tiny villages visible below on the lake. One of these is the town of Careno, the location of another historic lake lunch spot. Down in the town—and we mean *down*—is local treasure **Trattoria del Porto**. Reservations here are mandatory, and you must also call them when you're getting close to the town for instructions on where and how to park up on the road. After cracking that code, you walk down a couple hundred steep steps through the tiny streets of the ancient town until you arrive at the trattoria, which is perched another 100 feet or so above the water. All this work is worth it, though, as you'll be treated to a traditional menu that they have been serving for decades. Every day. The same menu. For decades. The fish dishes, especially—and there are several of them—are steeped in tradition of the lake's old families. The signature dish here is a plate of fried perch with rice dressed with butter and sage—simple, local, delicious. A boat dock below unloads visitors from all over the lake who come to Careno just to eat here. Next door to the restaurant is an unusual 11th-century church that has a porticoed anteroom looking out over the lake.

A bit farther north is the town of **Nesso**. The highway bisects the town. Above is the **Cascata Orrido**, the source of two rivers and a huge waterfall. Below is a picturesque old footbridge, **Ponte della Civera**, which crosses the river just before it flows into the lake. From Nesso, you can drive north to Bellagio, at the meeting of the two legs. Bellagio is not a huge town, but it's a highly manicured tourist spot. Our main interest here is taking a car ferry over to Varenna, at the top of the right leg of the lake. This triangular point of land, incidentally, is called the *triangolo lariano*, another vestige of the lake's original name.

You can choose to drive around the Larian triangle, or across it. If you do the latter, there are several little lakes in between the legs of Lake Como. One that may escape attention is the tiny

Lago di Segrino. This lake is a quiet retreat in the countryside, a preserved refuge for birds and other wildlife. A walking and biking path circles the whole lake, a total of about five kilometers. This is a perfect place to stretch your legs, or have a little picnic, away from the tourist crowds.

Make your way east to and around Lecco. This town is about the same size as Como and, like Como, it has many points of interest that are thoroughly covered in other guides. You'll cross the Fiume Adda into town. This river flows out of Lake Como and eventually joins the the Po River in Emilia Romagna.

Note that soon after leaving Lecco on the SS36, the road becomes a limited-access highway, so

look for an exit to SP72 towards Abbadia Lariana and Mandello del Lario. If you fail to make that junction, the SS36 will take you north through many kilometers of inescapable tunnels and exit-less highway, and you'll end up doing a lot of backtracking. (And also, if you're like us, cursing).

Mandello del Lario is another small town with a sizeable sprawl around it, but its *centro* has undeniable charm. The *piazza* at the *imbarcadero*, or boat dock, bustles with locals and visitors, many jostling for their turn to grab a treat at Gelateria Constantin. You can eat well and stay at **Mamma Ciccia**, in the heart of the old town. The owner, Silvia, runs an *albergo diffuso* and a cooking academy, so you can lodge at one of her distinctive properties in town and then take a class to learn how to make some traditional pastas and sauce (and tiramisu!). Better yet, her restaurant serves up delicious plates of standard fare, unfettered by the foibles of those who may not know their way around a pasta machine.

> ### Alberghi diffusi
> Over the past few decades, efforts to revitalize Italy's small historic towns have led to the rise of the *albergo diffuso* (literally, "scattered inn"). These are lodgings not in a single building like a standard hotel, but rather spread out in several of the town's old buildings. The result is an assortment of choices, from small B&B rooms to entire apartments, enabling travelers to immerse themselves into the local life of the town and feel like they're really living there.

Driving north on the SP72, you'll eventually arrive in **Varenna** (that is, if you didn't just take the boat across from Bellagio). The town itself has, among other items of interest, a beautiful botanical garden at the Villa Monastero, and also an Ornithological and Science Museum. Looming above the town is the **Castello di Vezio**, parts of which date back to the 12th century.

Farther north is Bellano, a town you may have already discovered accidentally, since it's the next place after Lecco to get off the highway. The town is best known for its **Orrido Bellano**, a footpath that leads to a bridge overlooking a huge waterfall, much like Nesso's *cascata* on the other side of the lake. Next, you'll come to the large town of Dervio, and then tiny Corenno Plinio, a medieval village carved into the rock. There's a 14th-century castle here. It's not open to visitors, but it's fun to see and walk around.

You'll finally arrive at the **Olgiasca peninsula**.

Follow signs to the town of the same name. (Keep a good eye out—it's a small place, and therefore small signs.) You can also look for signs to the **Abbazia di Santa Maria di Piona**, the old monastery at the very end of the peninsula. Here, again, we see the church's propensity for snagging all the best real estate. This 12th-century monastic settlement is impossibly beautiful, with perfectly kept gardens and an ancient stone church, all in the shadow of the imposing, snow-capped Alps. Better still, every evening at around 6:30, the monks hold a Gregorian chant service, which completes a visitor's transportation back in time. If you arrive earlier, the monks' shop may still be open, where they sell products made here, including a Piona herbal *liquore*.

Back up the hill in Olgiasca is the **Hotel Conca Azzurra**, flanked by palm trees in its incredible and ornate garden. Here you can eat a solid meal and stay in beautiful rooms or, for a slightly higher cost, one of the gorgeous nearby apartments with

balconies and patios.

North of this peninsula on the SP72 you'll pass through Colico. Just north of this town, history buffs will find a World War I site, the **Forte Montecchio Nord**. It was built in the early days of the war, as a heavily armed fortification on a hill overlooking the northern (*nord*) part of the lake. Visiting it is challenging, as it's open only on weekends and by appointment, but it is an impressive piece of history. Farther north, the road rejoins the larger SS36 and crosses the Adda River where it enters the top of Lake Como. Follow this up until it rejoins the water. You're now on the east side of Lago di Mezzola, a small lake near the top of Lake Como. Just before plunging into a tunnel, look for a little turn toward a *Galleria di*

Mina at **Verceia**. This is another WWI tunnel defense system (like the one at Brienno, described above) that was designed to be collapsed in the event of enemy advancement down this corridor from the north. Follow this narrow road along the water, down to a little residential area with a tiny park. This is a nice, quiet spot to sit for a few minutes and watch swans traverse the lake.

This little lake is connected to Lake Como by a small river, the Fiume Mera. Backtracking just a bit to the south, take the SP4 over to Ponte del Passo. Before crossing the bridge (*ponte*), turn left on Via Boschetto and follow it along the Mera to **Ristorante Beccaccino**. It seems counterintuitive to find such an upscale restaurant in such a remote location, but this family-run place has created a modern and beautiful dining space, and serves high-end cuisine, specializing, of course, in fish. A large and well-thought-out wine list accompanies your meal.

At this point you can cross the river and drive back down the west side of the lake to complete the circuit of Lake Como, or you can head east up the Adda valley and down toward Lago d'Iseo, our next route.

Isola Comacina

Locanda Comacina

Absolutely stellar, fixed price set meal, served the same way since 1948. Unmissable. Restaurant is closed November to beginning of March. During its open season, Tuesday is the closing day. Reservations recommended, as there may be special events that require a closing. 77€/pp, no credit cards. The boat ride is also paid in cash and is 8€/pp, paid at the boat.

https://www.comacina.it

Argegno

Gelato di Zoe

Artisanal gelateria in the town square. Open every day in summer, reduced hours in winter. Check their Facebook page for seasonal hours.

Careno

Trattoria del Porto

Traditional restaurant in a town that seems untouched by time, in part, because it's piled up on a cliff and not easy to navigate. Fixed price, same menu, every day. Amazing food. Book ahead, and ask for the table on the corner of the patio, which has stunning views of the lake. 26 Via Del Pontile, 22020 Careno CO, Italy. Phone: +39 031 910195

Mandello del Lario

Mamma Ciccia's

An enterprising family has created a whole industry in this town: restaurant, cooking school, and hotel. We took their cooking class and loved it. The restaurant is excellent and run by people who love food and care about tradition. Cooking class 65€/pp, reservations required.

https://www.mammaciccia.it/

Sorico

Ristorante Beccaccino

Upscale restaurant just north of Lake Como in a rural setting, specializing in sea and lake fish. Excellent wine list, well off the beaten track.

https://www.beccaccino.it/pubb/

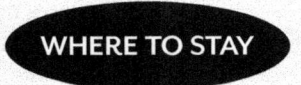

Carate Urio

Tiziana's Suite, Ai Cedri

Perfectly located vacation rentals on a quiet stretch of Lake Como. Tiziana's is a 2-bedroom apartment; Ai Cedri is larger, sleeping as many as 6. Off-street parking, stunning patio views.

https://www.airbnb.com/rooms/6457653
https://www.airbnb.com/rooms/24263430

Mandello del Lario

Mamma Ciccia's
Mamma Ciccia's is an *albergo diffuso*, with rooms scattered throughout the small town, whiich adds the effect of feeling like you live there. Zeneba had come down with a flu bug prior to arriving there, and they cared for her like family.

https://www.mammaciccia.it/

Olgiasca

Hotel Conca Azzurra
The only hotel in a quiet village perched above the lake. Several rooms have balconies; apartments available with kitchens and gardens. Restaurant on the ground floor of the hotel.

http://www.concazzurra.com/

Lenno

Oleificio Vanini Osvaldo
A little shop right where they bottle the oil, down a quiet street. They sell their famous oil here, also skin care products made with the oil. Open Monday - Saturday 8-12 and 1:30-6:30, Closed Sunday.

https://www.oliovanini.it/

Abbazia di Piona

Monk's Shop
The shop sells the famous liqueur and other items made by the monks. Open every weekday and on holidays; full hours here:

http://www.cistercensi.info/piona/

Varenna

Castello di Vezio
Castle with sweeping views of the lake. A falconry show offered in summer months. Closed November - March.

http://www.castellodivezio.it/

Olgiasca

Abbazia di Piona
Picture-perfect monastery at the end of the peninsula. Get there in the evening for their 6:30 PM Gregorian chant service.

https://www.abbaziadipiona.it/

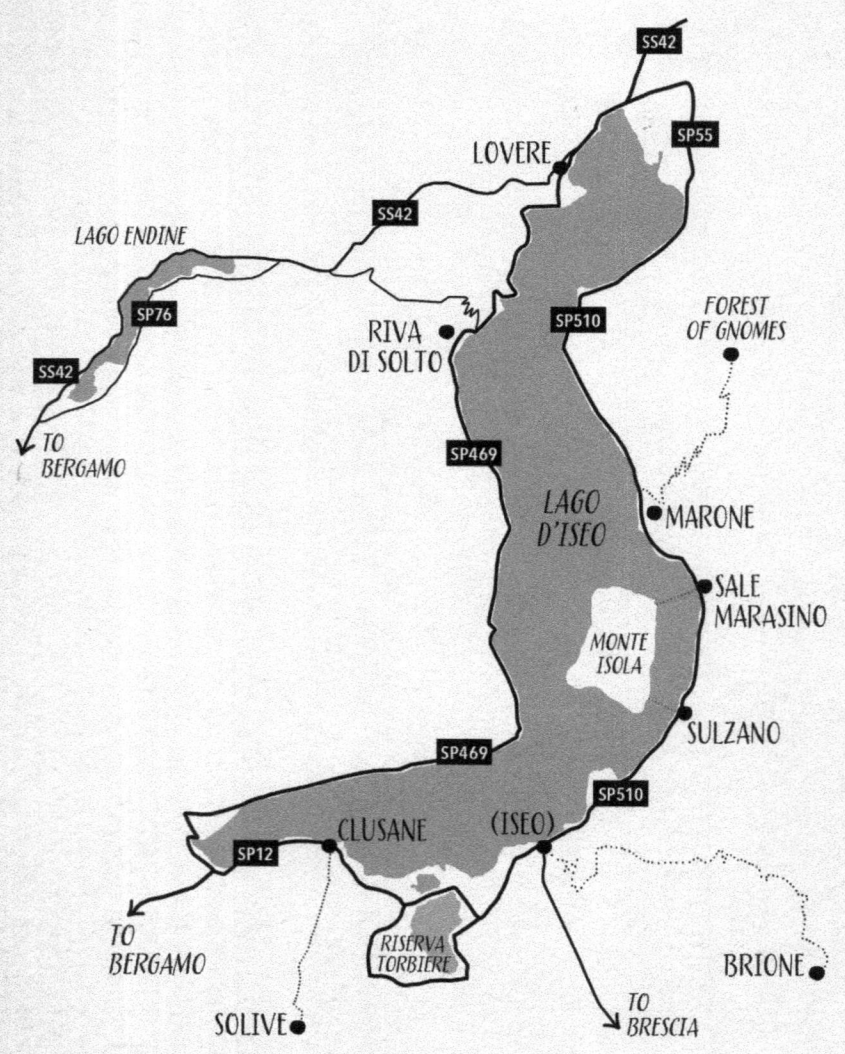

ROUTE #4

Lago d'Iseo

Iseo is Lombardy's fourth-largest lake, but it has a distinction all its own: It holds the largest lake island in Europe.

Whether you're approaching Lago d'Iseo from the north over the mountains, or coming up from Bergamo to the southwest, take a quick diversion to and around little **Lago d'Endine**. The SS42 is the bigger but nicer route, meandering along the western shoreline and giving drivers a gorgeous view across the lake to the lush green mountain park on the east side. The waters of this lake are an unbelievable color—metallic green or glassy gray or deep blue, depending on the weather and the time of day. Many roadside parking areas and picnic benches line the road, offering opportunities to stop for a photo or a snack. If you're lucky, you'll find a food truck serving up local goodies. A *panino* with local sausage and a beer hits the spot at one of these lakeside pull-offs.

Route #4 Lago d'Iseo

The highway passes through the town of Endine at the top of the lake and continues to Lovere, near the north end of Lago d'Iseo. This town is crowded but not too touristy, with a monumental and bustling central *piazza* by the lake. Lovere is home to several impressive and important churches: the huge 15th-century **Basilica di Santa Maria in Valvendra** on the north end of town; the **Santuario delle Sante Capitanio e Gerosa**, farther up the hill; and, higher up, past several blocks of residential neighborhoods, the small but enviably located **Chiesa di San Maurizio**,

which sits on a hill overlooking the town and lake. This is the church of an order of Franciscan Capuchin friars that has been here since the 15th century. Next to the church is a little chapel dedicated to Saint Peter, with a fresco depicting the Madonna and Child.

Coming back down the hill, find the main road through town, the SP469, locally known as the *Sebina Occidentale*. After passing through a less-than-picturesque modern industrial shipyard area, you'll abruptly find yourself on one of the most beautiful stretches of lakeside highway we've yet seen. The road hugs the cliffs close to the water as if its life depends on it—and yours does, so drive with caution here. Occasional short tunnels delve into the cliffs. You'll think you've stumbled upon a passage into the underworld, then suddenly emerge again to another breathtaking lake view. After about five kilometers, you'll see a little turn to **Riva di Solto**. Follow the side road into the village, which time and tourists seem to have largely forgotten. A tiny park on the lake makes for a local meeting spot, with a couple of cafes and a gelateria handy. A block farther down, the *birreria* **Tre Corone** is hidden on a side street. It has its own proprietary patio across the street right on the lake. Only two or three tables sit in this shady patio, so you have to be lucky with your timing. Tre Corone serves simple but high-quality sandwiches and plates, and they have a wide selection of really good beer, including some brews we'll visit more closely in Route 6. This restaurant and this village remind us of the little towns on the Amalfi coast—charming spots that are right by the water, but hidden and largely undiscovered.

A lovely half-hour drive (not including stops for photos and/or refreshments) south on the SP469 leads down to and around the south end of the lake, crossing the river Oglio at the town of Sarnico. Here the Oglio flows out of Lago Iseo to join the Po River in Emilia-Romagna. Shortly thereafter, catch the SP12 to the town of **Clusane**. On the edge of Clusane's *centro* is **Hostel del Gal** (attached to the Trattoria del Gallo). Free and easy parking, low prices, clean rooms, and proximity to the *centro* make this a good place to lodge for a night. It's an easy walk through the old town to the lakefront, where the natural landscape is complemented by the work of a local artist. Painted ceramic and metal sculptures are mounted in the little *piazza* here, as they are in towns all around the lake. This place feels like a

fishermen's village, and indeed, the practice of fishing here goes back to prehistoric times. Another block up the street is **Trattoria del Muliner**, an upscale but unfussy restaurant serving fine plates of traditional local dishes as well as some more creative modern fare. Needless to say, fish feature prominently on the menu.

This is the region of Franciacorta, a hilly area known for excellent wine production. Just a few kilometers straight south of Clusane, the farm of **Cascina Solive** is tucked away in the countryside. This agriturismo and restaurant is famous for its Franciacorta wine and its olive oil, as well as serving meals prepared from foodstuffs from their own farm and that of their neighbors. It doesn't get any more farm-to-table than this! The restaurant is large, but reservations are still recommended, since this place is regularly packed with locals.

Just southeast of Clusane is the **Riserva Naturale Torbiere del Sebino**, a vast wetland nature preserve with a network of boardwalk paths traversing the marsh, perfect for wildlife watchers and photographers. At the edge of this *riserva* is the thousand-year-old **Monastero di San Pietro**

in Lamosa, making this a good stop for history buffs as well as nature lovers.

Before proceeding north along the east side of Lake Iseo, another stop awaits that might be the oddest and most high-concept eatery we've ever visited. High up in the hills to the east of the town of Iseo (take SP48 to SP10, and then good luck finding the turn from there!) is **Trattoria La Madia**. From the little patio in front, the view is spectacular—the lake is down there somewhere amidst row after row of green mountains and sharp-cut valleys—and the food is unique. They specialize in sourcing all ingredients from local, sustainable providers, and also in fermenting things. Lots of things. Their anteroom is overflowing with jars filled with all manner of pickled goods. Your meal will likely begin with an amuse-bouche of a fermented drink or

foodstuff, to set the tone. Unusual flavor combinations are the norm. La Madia seeks to expand diners' palates with inventive blends of tastes, smells, and textures. Each dish is presented at table with a detailed explanation, and questions are encouraged. This is a place for eco-conscious and adventurous eaters. It's extremely popular for visitors and locals alike, so calling ahead for a reservation is a must.

Returning to Iseo, proceed north along the lake road. Not the SP510, which is another of those faster, limited-access highways that will bypass much of the good lakeside driving. (If you do get stuck on that highway, exit at Sulzano and get down to the lake that way.) Sulzano is a bustling town on the lake. Continuing up the lake road you'll pass the Blue Marlin birreria and pizzeria on the outskirts of the village of **Sale Marasino**. Toward the center of town, look for **Casa Salini**, a lovely little lakeside B&B. Guests have use of the lake-level garden (you can even jump in for a swim!), as well as a common room that's bursting with books and comfortable couches, giving the place a "just like living there" vibe. Signora Salini herself lives on site, but you never see her except when you need her, like when she serves you breakfast on the sunny terrace with sweeping views of the lake.

Just north of this house on the right as you exit the town is a simple-looking roadside shop. This is **Pasticceria Briola 1955**, a fantastic and artistic family-run bakery that, as the name implies, has been in business for decades. Try their exquisitely crafted macarons, or have a cappuccino and a *petit four* on their patio on your way to catch the boat or drive up the mountain. Locals stop in for house-made gelato, croissants, or loaves of crusty bread. We will go well out of our way to stop here. Grab a treat to nibble on your way up the mountain or to take back to your lodging for later.

Speaking of driving up the mountain: A bit farther north brings you to the town of Marone, above which are two little villages, Pregasso and Zone, each containing sites that are unforgettable in different ways. Outside of Zone (pronounced ZOH-nay), whimsy is on display in the **Bosco di Gnomi**, or "Forest of Gnomes." Paths leading through the woods are scattered with hand-carved gnomes and other fantastical creatures. This is a fun, "hidden" place for kids of all ages, as long as they're prepared to walk a lot. In Pregasso, you'll find the initial stone steps of a *Via Crucis*, a Stations of the Cross path that leads up the mountain to the **Eremo di San Pietro**. Not only is this great exercise (which may or may not be a good thing, depending on how long you lingered at the *pasticceria*), but your devotion to the ascent rewards you with the most stunning view of the lake and its island, Montisola.

From either Sale Marasino or from Sulzano, you can leave the car for a few hours or a few days and take a boat to the center—and the centerpiece—of the lake: **Monte Isola** (or Montisola), the largest lake-island in Europe.

For overnight parking, you can try to find free spots in the neighborhoods (denoted by white lines), or you can ask at a bar about parking lots with cheap daily rates. Both towns have these options.

Montisola is essentially a single mountain—hence the name—at the peak of which is the **Santuario della Madonna della Ceriola**. This monastic settlement was founded in the fifth century, and has been vital to the region's spirituality ever since. It has been built upon and improved over the centuries (the "current" sanctuary dates from the early 1600s), but it remains a timeless haven for pilgrims and pagan visitors alike. The only way up is to walk the steep *Via Crucis* from the little hamlet of Curé near the top of the mountain, about 275 meters up from the lake shore level.

Montisola is vaguely rectangular in shape, and has towns on the water at its four "points," as well as several up in the hills. They're all connected by narrow roads and by a mini-bus service, but most of the roads are easily walkable around the lake edge. (Cars are not permitted on the island except, as the law dictates, for doctors and priests. From the looks of things, the island must have an awful lot of doctors and priests....)

At the northeast corner (closest to Sale Marasino) is **Carzano**, with several shops and restaurants and a nice beach area for swimming. Walking clockwise around the island, it's about two kilometers down to **Peschiera Maraglio**, the island's biggest town. Its church of San Michele Arcangelo is a block off of the water. In this case, at least, the best real estate belongs to the fishermen and shopkeepers. On this lake walk, especially on the south edge of the island, you'll see racks of *agoni* splayed and hanging in the sun, as prescribed by the traditional month-long drying process to preserve and prepare these fish. The tradition has been captured by a local artist, whose metal and ceramic artworks are installed all around the lake. It's fun to see how close you have to get to tell the art from the real thing.

There are many lovely little cafes and bars along this strip, making it easy to find a picturesque coffee or cocktail. At the end of town, facing south, is **La Foresta**, a simple but lovely hotel and the best restaurant on the island (with one possible exception forthcoming). Some of the rooms have balconies looking out over the lake, and the cuisine here is, of course centered around expert preparations of lake fish. But ichthyophobes can still expect to be well-fed here: La Foresta also serves a *salame di Montisola*, a cured meat that's produced on the island, as well as handmade pastas based on *terra firma*.

Another kilometer or so clockwise around the island brings us to the **Colonia Felina Gatti al Sole**—a feral cat colony. Townspeople have set up a portion of the lakeside woods with shelters, water sources, and food stations so the island's cats can take refuge from the elements. Just a bit farther is the town of **Sensole**, the westernmost point of the island. Here you can find a couple of lodgings and restaurants, including **Ristorante Vittoria**, whose diners enjoy a beautiful lakeside patio. Above the town is the 14th-century Castello Oldofredi, once the dominant watchtower fortification for the south and west parts of the lake.

The walk from Peschiera Maraglio to Sensole is flat and easy. More ambitious hikers may continue on foot to Siviano. If you want a more relaxing trip, you can take the boat around the island, which offers beautiful views in all directions. A note to walkers: While there are small shops and bars in the little towns on the mountain, hours of operation vary, so bring water or snacks. You'll find plenty of benches and even some picnic tables on the walking paths in the hills.

Iseo's Little Islands

Two tiny islands sit at either end of the larger island of Montisola. Isola di San Polo was home to a monastery for hundreds of years beginning in the 11th century. The monks were ejected in the 18th century and the island became private property, as it remains today. To the north of Montisola is Isola di Loreto, where a sister convent was established at the same time monks occupied San Polo. The sisters abandoned it after a few centuries. In the early 1900s a castle was built upon the ruins. Although both islands are private and closed to visitors, they add an extra bit of picturesque mystery to the vistas on the lake.

Continuing clockwise around the island, you'll leave the lake shore and ascend to the village of Menzino. From here, one road leads to Senzano and up to Curé, from which point you can walk up to the *santuario*. The other road leads north to continue the circle (or rather, the rectangle) of the island to the picturesque village of **Siviano** on the northwest "corner" of the island, high up on the hill above the water. This town has a little central *piazza* and a bar overlooking the lake that's often filled with old local guys playing cards and drinking espresso and grappa.

Route #4 Lago d'Iseo

A tiny path leads down the hill to the lake's edge, where an even tinier cluster of houses and other buildings sit. This is Siviano's "port," and the vital connection to the town above. Just a short walk along the lake from the *imbarcadero*, the dining area of the incredible **Locanda Canogola** sits right on the lake. This is a family restaurant operated by the sister of the woman who operates La Foresta in Peschiera Maraglio. The culinary gift clearly runs in the family, and you'll find traditional, fresh, local lake cuisine, perfectly prepared. Reservations are a must, as the restaurant

often will not open unless they know they have incoming guests, even in high season. You'll feel like family when you eat here. It's that kind of atmosphere, as if you're guests in their house.

But you won't need to actually stay in their house if you book the beautiful **Villetta Floriana**, just a block away and also right on the water. It's a gorgeous house with a kitchen, a little balcony off the bedroom and, best of all, a patio with a flowery garden and lawn overlooking the lake. Floriana will greet you when you get off the boat, walk you to the house, show you around, and then leave

you on your own to really experience the luxury of living here. For us, "luxury" isn't about being waited on hand and foot. Luxury, for us, is taking possession of a heavenly slice of real estate that  we get all to ourselves where we can drink wine, watch the sunset, and pretend we are locals in a peaceful place that seems too beautiful to be on earth.

WHERE TO EAT

Clusane

Trattoria del Muliner
Fantastic family-run restaurant specializing in lake fish and traditional recipes of Lago Iseo, just a few steps from the lake itself. Reservations recommended. Closed Tuesdays.

http://www.trattoriadelmuliner.it/

Corte Franca

Solive
Solive is one-stop shopping for the foodie traveler. An excellent restaurant here, comfortable rooms in the B&B, wine and oil for sale to take home, and even a small "Farmer's Museum" on site. Restaurant open for lunch on Monday, lunch and dinner Wednesday - Sunday. Closed Tuesday, and Monday night.

https://solive.it/

Riva di Solto

Tre Corone
Cute pub with light snacks and a lovely outdoor space right on the lake; large selection of local and foreign draft beers. Closed Thursday.

http://trecoronepub.it/

Brione

Trattoria la Madia
A mountaintop trattoria for adventurous eaters, especially those interested in fermentation. Open for dinner Wednesday - Friday; lunch and dinner Saturday and Sunday. Closed Monday and Tuesday.

https://www.trattorialamadia.it/

Sale Marasino

Pasticceria Briola 1955
Absolutely incredible bakery, table service on the patio. Don't miss this place if you like sweets. Open Tuesday - Sunday 6:30am-8pm. Closed Monday.

https://www.facebook.com/Briola.1955/

Peschiera Maraglio

La Foresta
Well-known excellent restaurant on Montisola, specializing in lake fish. In warmer months, ask for a table on their beautiful patio. Closed late December - March, and Wednesdays.

http://www.forestamontisola.it/

Siviano

Locanda Canogola
The sister of the owner of Foresta owns this lovely "hidden" spot; make sure to book ahead to avoid disappointment as it is well off the beaten track.

http://www.canogola.it/

Clusane

Hostel del Gal
Sometimes we choose a place because it's easy to park there, and it's close to an important restaurant. This is one of those—simple, immaculate, affordable, and a friendly staff.

https://www.hosteldelgal.com/

Sale Marasino

B&B Casa Salini
A gorgeous house on the lake with a few rooms; two have balconies. The friendly Signora Salini serves breakfast on the terrace overlooking the lake.

http://www.casasalini.it

Siviano

Villetta Floriana
A stand-alone house, master bedroom with balcony, front garden with table and chairs, all overlooking the lake. A quiet, beautiful paradise too beautiful to believe. As of 2018 there is a outdoor cat named "Grigio" who *will* want to get some attention and snacks from you.

https://www.airbnb.com/rooms/10099779

Peschiera Maraglio

La Foresta
Several rooms upstairs from their excellent restaurant—do yourself a favor and get one of the ones with a balcony, to enjoy a private sunset show.

http://www.forestamontisola.it/

ROUTE #5

Lago di Garda

Garda is the biggest lake in Italy, larger than Maggiore and Como combined. Its surrounding roads connect hubs of tourism to wild natural areas—and countless small towns and historical sites abound in between.

To the north of Lago d'Idro (west of Lago di Garda) is Storo, a small town well known for its production of a particular yellow cornmeal. Just outside the town, surrounded by vineyards and nestled among towering pre-alpine peaks, is the beautiful **Agriturismo La Polentera**, whose menu

specializes in polenta made from the golden Storo yellow flour. B&B guests also receive a welcome tray of delicious cookies made with this prized food commodity. This place is another perfect example of a lodging where travelers can eat extraordinarily well and then just roll themselves up to their cozy and comfortable rooms. The *agriturismo* serves as an informal art gallery, as well—both the rooms and the restaurant are decorated with intricate and creative hand-carved wood sculptures by a local artist.

Polenta

Ever since European colonizers introduced corn from the Americas to Europe, polenta has been one of the main staples of northern Italian cooking. Made from cornmeal, it comes in many forms and is used in many different dishes. A fine grind might be used to create a mashed-potato type of dish, while the coarser grains might be used for bread-like sides. Polenta also becomes a pasta substitute, a vehicle for sauces of meats, cheeses, or vegetables. It's sometimes even incorporated into desserts. The carefully-cultivated corn in the fields around Storo (north of Lago d'Idro) yields the unique Storo yellow flour, which makes especially delicious polenta.

Lake Idro itself is the highest of these Italian lakes in this region, and indeed the hills here are so steep that only the west side of the lake is passable by car. About halfway down on the SS237 is the **Rocca d'Anfo**, a 15th-century castle that was subsequently improved and used by Napoleon and then by Italian forces in both World Wars. The site is now a popular tourist attraction, with guided tours that must be booked in advance. If the crowds are too much for you, take a few moments to explore the lakeside park in Anfo town, where you can see the castle in peace from a distance and have an espresso at the little beachside bar.

At the south end of the lake is the sleepy lakeside town of Lemprato. From here, follow the winding SP111 road south up into the hills. On the way up there's a pull-off area with a bench facing a spectacular view of the lake and the snow-

Route #5 Lago di Garda

capped Alps beyond. This road ends at the SP56 highway, which leads east to the tiny hamlet of Vico and the excellent **Locanda Lamarta**. Run by the same family for more than a century, this restaurant has no menus, but proudly serves traditional cuisine made by what is locally available in season. The cozy dining room is filled with books and family heirlooms, and often has a log fire burning on the hearth. Each course will have one or two options, which the server will enumerate at table. Be sure to start with a plate of their house-made salumi.

Route #5 Lago di Garda

There are roads that lead east from here over the hills, but they are meandering and precipitous. An easier path lies back to the north from Storo, and leads to a tiny but beautiful lake. Drive east from Storo on the SS240 and you'll reach Lago di Ledro, ringed by quiet little villages with a handful of restaurants, lodgings, and shops. Just east of Mezzolago (literally "half-lake") is a peaceful hilltop lodging, **B&B Ai Casai**. Owner Michaela and her family live in this house, but her guests enjoy immaculate private rooms

Bagoss cheese

Unique to the hills within the *comune* of Bagolino, near Lago d'Idro, Bagoss is the result of centuries of pastoral cheesemaking traditions and skill. Milk comes from cows that dine only on certain alpine pastures, on their particular grasses and herbs. It takes about 300 liters of milk to make one wheel of cheese—the remnants are made into alpine butter. Only a few dozen alpine cheesemaking locations in the area are authorized to make bagoss. Production is limited; the process is time-consuming and highly detailed; and the results are precious 35-pound wheels of aged deliciousness.

Route #5 Lago di Garda

and an expansive lawn with a wisteria-draped pergola that overlooks the vivid aquamarine lake and its surrounding mountains. When we find a remote lodging like this with such a beautiful view, we like to arrive stocked with local groceries so we can create our own picnic dinner. (Don't forget the wine!) This accomplishes three goals: Eat locally, eat affordably, and relax. This is a perfect place to retreat from the bustle of Italy's largest lake, Lago di Garda.

The SS240 leads to Riva del Garda, the town at the top of the Lake Garda. This large, sprawling town is home to a lakeside castle museum. A short walk from the *centro* leads through the woods up to the Bastione di Garda, a 16th-century tower that overlooks the town's harbor.

Route #5 Lago di Garda

The east side of Lake Garda, along the SR249, is generally more extensively developed for tourism—more towns, more hotels, more beaches and centers of water sports, and even a couple of amusement parks. It's a popular spot for German tourists, as it lies almost directly on the autostrada that comes from Munich through Austria. This side is crowded with sporty people, doing sporty things at sporty facilities like parasailing and kayaking and (we assume) water-climbing and surf-lifting. We tend to prefer glass-hoisting, fork-balancing, and stomach-filling, but to each their own!

Route #5 Lago di Garda

In any case, we can still find some nice things to do on this side without breaking much of a sweat. The ancient Scaligeri family were, for centuries, the rulers of Verona and its territory, which included Lake Garda. Consequently, several "Scaliger castles" sit on this east side of the lake. One is the Malcesine castle, in the town of the same name; another is further south on the lakeside road in Torri del Benaco. About halfway between these two sites is Pai, a tiny town high above the lake edge. Here you can stay at the **Locanda San Marco**, a nice, simple restaurant lodging.

Across the town square is a path leading up to the town's church, which has a little "hidden" terrace overlooking the bustling towns on the lake below. This is a convenient and peaceful place to stay that's close to the lakeside without being right in the center of it all.

Farther south on the SR249 are several more busy towns (including Garda itself), and also several water parks, an aquarium, and "Gardaland," which is sort of a Disneyland of northern Italy, but without Mickey Mouse. Needless to say, these places are not exactly "Little Roads" destinations, so we'll give them a pass and take a look at the west side of Lake Garda.

From Riva del Garda, follow the SS45-bis highway. You'll plunge through tunnels and cling to the lakes' edge on your way to **Limone sul Garda**. This town, as the name implies, is famous for growing lemons. Walk down into the old *centro* and visit **La Limonaia del Castel**, an open-air museum and terraced lemon grove that provides an interesting history of the town and its lemony traditions, as well as a constant scent of citrus tree flowers wafting through the air. A few more blocks down leads you to the water's edge and the excellent **Hotel Ristorante Monte Baldo**. A well-

timed call in advance will score you a table on the little balcony overlooking the town's old boat quay, where you can enjoy expertly prepared dishes while the crowds mill below you. And since lemons grow abundantly here, you can get a fantastic local *limoncello* and a water view with‑
out the crowds and the prices of the Amalfi Coast.

From Limone, you can continue south on the lakeside highway, or divert to the SP38 road, on which you can twist your way slowly but surely to the entrance of the **Santuario di Montecastello**. The sanctuary, dating from the 16th century but built on the site of an earlier Christian temple (c. 800 AD), sits atop a towering limestone outcropping in the mountainside. The road up to this hermitage church is lined with shrines creating a *Via Crucis*—the Stations of the Cross. Walking (or driving, if your car is small enough) to the top rewards

pilgrims of any spiritual leanings with an incredible view of the lake. It speaks volumes of the devotion—and the resources—of the strong souls who built this religious stronghold in such a precipitous location centuries ago. More modern devotees can refresh themselves with a coffee or other beverage at the little bar next to the entrance to the grounds. Religious or not, taking in the view from such an extreme height at the lake is a profound experience. The water and the sky seem to meld together, and you'll feel as if you're looking down from some heavenly position. As with many such vistas among these pre-alpine

lakes, this one reminds us of standing on a coastal cliff in Ireland, but with placid lake water in place of the turbulent ocean.

From here, that same SP38 road leads back down to the lake. On the way is the town of Gardola, where the modest but friendly **B&B Miramonti** offers little terrace rooms above their pizzeria. Down the street is **Osteria La Miniera**, which serves up traditional dishes of the region including—of course!—lake fish based on the day's catch.

The lake road continues further south past a few more towns before arriving at Gardone Riviera, which we'll return to in a moment. For now, continue south. To get around the larger, more modern and commercial town of Salò, catch the SP572 road, which continues to the other end of Lake Garda. Follow signs to the east for **Riserva Naturale della Rocca di Manerba** (or some combination of these words, as Italian signage is not the most reliable). This park offers a broad swath of the area's history, with ample signage describing the many settlement structures built here over the millenia. The site contains ruins from prehistoric epochs to Roman times to the medieval period. All of it was built on a hilltop with sweeping views of the lake to the north, east and south. A cross now sits atop the highest point here, which again speaks to the church's devotion (and its ability to corner the best real estate).

The town of **Gardone Riviera** is a little stretch of upscale lakeside luxury without the upscale prices. A beautiful and flowerful pedestrian zone runs along the water, flanked by a row of cute cafes and restaurants. One such is attached to the family-run **Hotel Diana**, whose rooms have enviable yet affordable balconies overlooking the lake and the promenade. This is a good place to catch the boat service from Gardone to, among other places, the Sirmione peninsula, which juts into the lake from its southern edge. **Sirmione** is the excavation site of an ancient Roman villa, as well as the home of another Scaliger castle. It has always been a crowded tourist attraction, limited as it is by its narrow geography, and since it was one setting in the film *Call Me By Your Name*, the crowds here are now even more daunting. Still, it's an incredible bit of history. (Note: A boat service operates on Lake Garda—*Navigazione Lago di Garda*—providing passenger transportation between many of the towns mentioned above.)

If staying put in Gardone is more your speed, you're in luck: A short but steep walk up the hill from the lake is the Heller Garden, a lush and extravagant botanical garden and open-air museum. Still farther up is **Il Fiore di Zucca** (literally "pumpkin flower"), a restaurant specializing in Roman cuisine. Fried zucchini flowers are always on the menu. Sit on their beautiful patio and enjoy a culinary evening in Rome. Your steep walk up rewards you with a quiet dining experience, far away from the lakeside crowds; and fortunately, it's all downhill as you tromp back to your hotel on the lake.

Storo

Agriturismo La Polentera
Specializing in polenta, specifically the famous yellow corn polenta of Storo. Try polenta in all its forms — including dessert! Open for lunch and dinner Wednesday through Monday; closed Tuesday.

http://www.lapolentera.it/

Treviso Bresciano

Locanda Lamarta
Absolutely gorgeous, evocative place to have a traditional lunch. Reservations required, as they may not open if they don't have bookings. Closed Thursdays.

http://www.lamarta.info/

Limone Sul Garda

Hotel Ristorante Monte Baldo
Upscale modern Italian cuisine in a beautiful restaurant right on the quay. Three tables on the balcony. Open seasonally, so book ahead to avoid disappointment.

https://www.montebaldolimone.it/portal/en/.html

Gardola

Osteria La Miniera
Cozy and charming, serving up traditional cuisine from the lake and the territory. Open for lunch and dinner every day except Tuesday.

http://www.gardaminiera.it/index.php?lang=en

Gardone Riviera

Il Fiore di Zucca
Specializing in Roman cuisine, up the hill above the lake. Open for lunch and dinner every day except Tuesday.
http://www.ilfioredizucca.it/

Mezzolago

B&B Ai Casai
The most stunning fairy-tale view over the lake. Two elegant rooms, although the owner plans to expand soon. Cash only.
http://www.ledroholiday.it/en-us/p/6/b-b-ai-casai

Pai

Locanda San Marco
A cute little hotel above a pizzeria restaurant, on a hill above the lake. A small-town alternative to the bigger resort hotels on the water.
http://www.locandasanmarco.it/

Gardola

B&B Miramonti
Above a pizzeria/bar. One of the most affordable places in this book. The rooms are basic but immaculate. Some rooms have balconies. Hint: Order a cocktail at the bar and take it to your room to enjoy on the balcony!
http://www.miramontihoteltignale.com/

Gardone Riviera

Hotel Diana
Surprisingly affordable, rooms with balconies right on the water. Small, family-run hotel in an excellent location.
https://www.dianagardone.it/

Storo

Agriturismo La Polentera
Idyllic mountain setting, lovely rooms, fantastic restaurant attached. (See listing above in Where to Eat)
http://www.lapolentera.it/

Limone Sul Garda

La Limonaia del Castel
Charming citrus garden in the center of town. Take a walk through the citrus gardens and learn a little local history too. 2€/pp. Hours vary by season, so check this link:
https://www.visitlimonesulgarda.com/

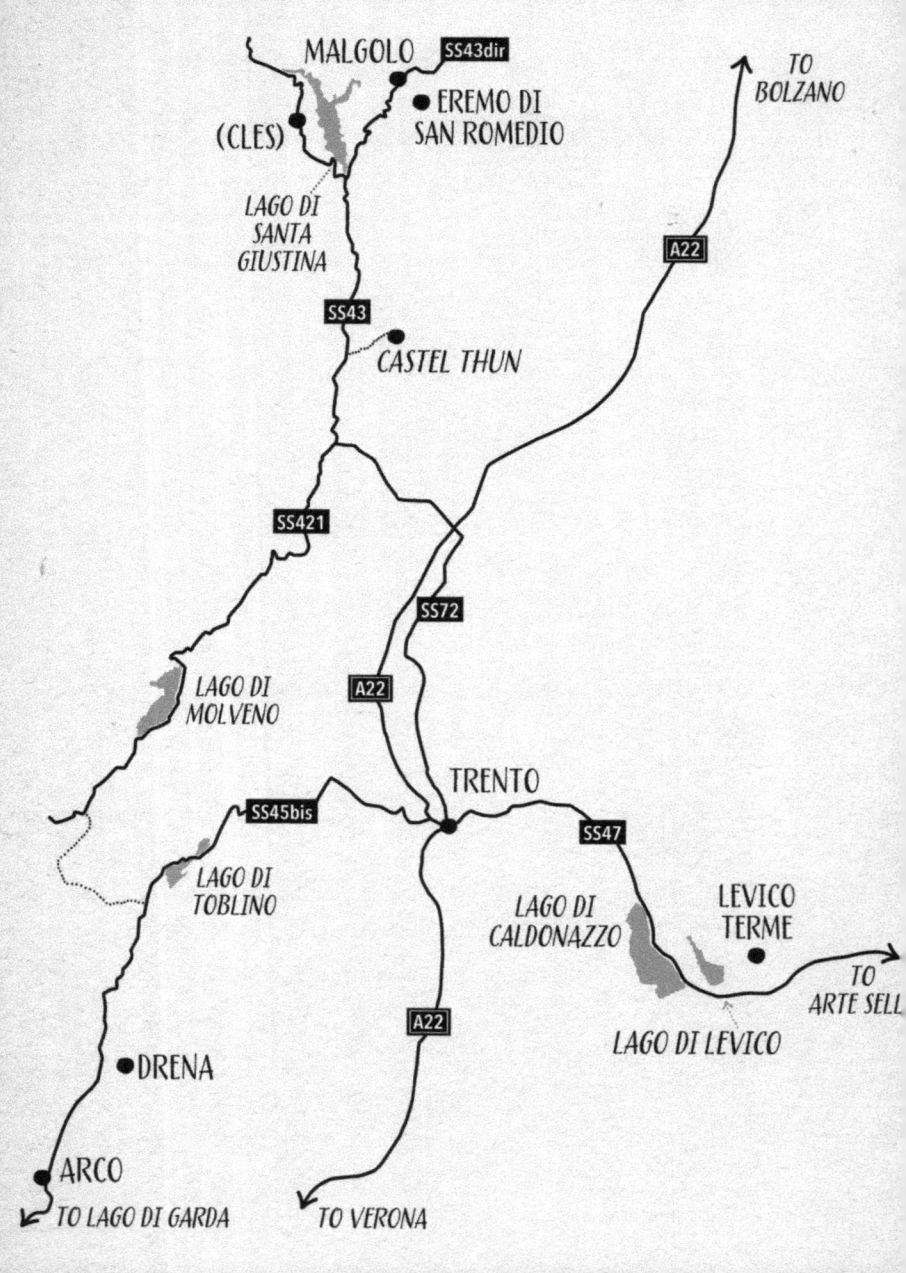

ROUTE #6

The Trentino

This region north of Lago di Garda is not centered around any big lake, though there are numerous small ones up here, tucked in between mountains and castles. In this route we explore sites centered around these little lakes.

In this mountain territory, there are dozens of castles perched on cliffs, with the snow-capped peaks of the Alps as a stunning backdrop. Villages here have that "mountain chalet" feel—ornately carved balcony railings, pointed rooftops, abundant firewood stacked perfectly. This is the Südtirol (South Tyrol) region, which was once part of the Austrian Empire.

Just north of Lake Garda, the highway changes route numbers frequently, but it follows the path of Fiume Sarca, one of the principal rivers feeding the lake from the Alps. Eventually the road settles on SS45bis, and comes to Arco. This town's old *centro* is picturesque in its own right, but it is distinctive for its position at the bottom of a huge cliff

face. A 20-minute walk up a well-maintained but steep path brings you to the **Castello di Arco** at the top of the cliff. One huge tower looms over the town, and another even higher one looks out over the river and the valley beyond. This is one of the most impressive hilltop castle sites in the region, for its history and for the sheer audacity of building something like this on such a precipice.

Farther up the valley is the town of Dro. From here, divert up the eastern slope to **Castello Drena**, another medieval fortress ruin. It's not as impressive a position as that at Arco, but just as impressive a structure.

Continuing along the SS45bis, we come to two tiny interconnected lakes, Lago di Santa Massenza and Lago di Toblino. On the latter, a little peninsula sticks out into the turquoise waters. It's an island, really, since a tiny canal was created where the land once touched the shore. On the island sits the fairytale-worthy **Castel Toblino**. Crenellated

Route #6 The Trentino

walls encircle the property, a round tower looks out over the lake, and the gardens next to the castle are fragrantly flowerful and woodsy. A walking path along the lake's edge offers beautiful views. On a clear day, the castle and the surrounding hills are mirrored perfectly on the still lake surface. The castle isn't open to visitors … unless you want to eat there, in which case you're in luck! This is one of our all-time favorite restaurants, both for its location and for its upscale and delicious cuisine.

Route #6 The Trentino

Our northward trek is enhanced by a bit of a diversion. Just south of Lake Toblino, catch the SS237 in Sarche and take that west to the SS421. This will head north again, along a beautiful stretch of mountain road. One stretch of this scenic route runs along the stunning and deserted Lago di Molveno. Another passes through the village of Castel Belfort, the site of—you guessed it—**Castel Belfort**, another medieval castle ruin. Farther still, the road joins the SS43, which follows the Torrente Noce (another river feeding Lake Garda) up to Lago di Santa Giustina and the town of Cles.

In Cles, on the west side of the lake, there's another castle, looking across the water to Malgolo. You reach Malgolo by taking the SS43dir at the foot of this lake up the east bank. There's a castle here as well, and we imagine the rivalry between local lords in this region must have been intense. (Which duke has the best castle? Whose is highest, or biggest, or fanciest? We'd guess, looking at the long game, that the ones that are still privately owned and lived in are the winners.)

In Malgolo, you'll find **Albergo Ristorante Nerina**—a slow food restaurant, whose menu lists the farms, cheesemakers, and butchers from whom they source their ingredients. This is another family-run place, serving traditional dishes of the highest quality but without pomp or fuss, in an adorable setting that feels like grandma's dining room. Upstairs from the restaurant is a hotel with modest but immaculate rooms, some of which have balconies overlooking a vast acreage of apple orchards, with mountains beyond. We have a soft spot in our hearts for this

Apples of the Trentino

The Trentino is highly-regarded for its fruit production— ciliege (cherries), fragole (strawberries), more (blackberries), lamponi (raspberries), mirtilli (blueberries), susine (plums), and especially *mele*—apples. In particular, the region of the Noce River valley and Lake Santa Giustina is flush with apple orchards that produce some of the country's most prized fruit. They appear as ingredients in any number of dishes, including a Trentino apple strudel— a traditional dish with a culinary connection in Austria, to which the Trentino once belonged.

hotel/restaurant; the very first time we came here, we were so enthusiastically greeted when we checked in that we felt like a part of the family.

Coming back down the SS43dir road, look for a turnoff in Sanzeno for the thousand-year-old monastic settlement of **Eremo di San Romedio**. A series of winding roads will lead you to this hidden hermitage ensconced in a forest valley. There's also a precipitous walking path up from the town. (When we visited this place, our GPS device led us to this site via some impossibly steep and twisting dirt roads. We ultimately arrived by car on what was essentially a walking path or fire road, much to the consternation of the other visitors there. We make these mistakes so you don't have to. You're welcome!)

Aside from its staggeringly tall bell tower and pointed rooftops jutting out of the valley, its several churches piled together on the steep valley wall, and the medieval frescoes on the walls inside and out, San Romedio is famous for a

peculiar resident, Bruno the bear. Legend has it that the fourth-century saint Romedius encountered a bear in his pilgrimage travels. The bear killed his horse, so Romedius tamed the bear and rode it instead. In the 20th century, an injured bear slated for extermination was given to the hermitage, where the monks built an enclosure and cared for him. Since then, this has been the home of a bear that would otherwise have been killed.

Heading back south on the SS43, you'll pass the impressive **Castel Thun**, one of several historical strongholds of the powerful Buonconsiglio rulers. Their seat of power was in **Trento**, to which we arrive presently.

This is the biggest town we visit in this guide, though it's generally considered a "small" town by many standards. Paid parking is cheap in a town like this, so don't spend time looking for a free lot. The few euro are well worth it, weighed against the extra time you'll want to have for sightseeing here.

Work your way to the **Castello di Buoncon-**

siglio, the main seat of power of the ruling dynasty of Trento. This was a 13th-century castle that was subsequently expanded and fortified. The castle has dozens of rooms containing a wealth of artworks and displays of, well, wealth. The Venetian Gothic loggia on the third floor boasts sweeping views of the valley below, and you can be forgiven for thinking just for a moment that you're in Venice. The castle is remarkable for its Torre Aquila ("Eagle Tower"), a relatively small

part of the residence containing a series of 15th-century frescoes depicting each month of the year. The frescoes illustrate medieval life in each season, for royalty and peasants. It is worth noting that the peasants are always small in size, while the aristocracy are depicted quite large, symbolic of their perceived importance. One of the scenes is singular: the first large-scale depiction of a winter scene in European art. (And it's a snowball fight!) Make sure you buy the ticket that includes this tower tour when you enter the castle—it's a quick tour, but it's unique, and it comes with an informative audio guide.

Trento has a lot to see. Several beautiful civic parks offer frequent green space amidst the city streets. Its huge *duomo*, the **Cattedrale di San Vigilio**, was built atop an old sixth-century church dedicated to Saint Vigilius. Inside the cathedral, on the south wall, is a "staircase to nowhere" … we had to restrain ourselves from climbing to the top. The *piazza* here has a huge fountain, the Fontana di Nettuno, which is reminiscent of the

Trevi in Rome. A block away is an archaeological museum displaying parts of the ancient Roman city buried beneath the modern Trento.

A couple of blocks south of the *piazza duomo* is **Antica Birreria Pedavena**. This is not just a *birreria*—a place where they serve beer in abundance—but a *birrificio*, where they actually make the stuff. Pedavena one of Italy's most highly regarded craft breweries. The food is pub fare, Tyrol-style: a mix of Germanic and Italian traditions that U.S. travelers will find familiar indeed. Pedavena has a beautiful, flowery beer garden you can enjoy in warmer months, but be sure to take a personal tour of the dining room, which is like a little museum with its walls full of local photos and historical artifacts.

Cesare Battisti

The Trentino region of Italy is full of memorials and tributes to the Austrian scholar and politician Cesare Battisti, a hero of the land. He was from Trento, which in his time was part of Austria. He agitated for this region to become part of Italy during WWI. For this, the Austrians executed him in 1916 at Trento's Castello Buonconsiglio.

Two years later the war ended, and much of the southern Austrian territory was ceded to Italy after all, including the Trentino and the Südtirol. Today, the towering columns of a mausoleum overlooks the castle from a nearby mountain-top, memorializing Battisti's legacy as the man who brought Trentino into the Italian republic.

From the castle—indeed, from many points in the *centro*—you can see a monument up on a hill across the river. This is part of a memorial park, **Parco Naturale del Doss Trento**, dedicated to Cesare Battisti, and includes old World War I cannons and a mausoleum. Battisti was a hometown boy and a hero of the Trentino. He was executed at Buonconsiglio Castle, which makes all the more sweet this monument's position looking down from a height onto the former seat of power.

Head southeast out of Trento to get to the vicinity of another pair of small lakes: Lago di Caldonazzo and Lago di Lévico. Take the SS47 east for a good while. At Borgo Valsugana, look for signs to Sella. (This seems far afield, and it is, but it's worth the diversion, we promise.) Snow-capped Alpine mountains poke above the tops of trees everywhere you look. After a good stretch of nothing but woods and hills, you'll come to a large park area that's dedicated to an outdoor art project, **Arte Sella**. There are several sections of this park, with different installations, and a good bit of walking is required, though none of it is too strenuous.

The art here is made from either natural or reclaimed wood and stone, and the installations change often, either with the addition of new artists,

or simply due to the fact that some of the art is reclaimed by the earth itself. It's a gorgeous idea that celebrates both creativity and sustainability. You could spend an hour here or an entire day, depending on how much you want to walk.

Returning to the aforementioned pair of lakes, we go up the hill to the town of **Levico Terme**, above Lake Lévico. The little *centro* is charming and bustling with shops, street vendors, and cafes.

Route #6 The Trentino

The **Hotel Antica Rosa** is a block from the central *piazza* with its big clock tower and the wide steps up to the **Chiesa di Santissimo Redentore**. The hotel is old but well-kept, and one room has a tiny little balcony looking out at the tower. Down the street a couple of blocks, **Ponte dei Sapori** wine shop offers a treasure trove of local wines, *liquori*, and other locally produced foodstuffs, including bags of dried apples and grappa made from green apples of the region. The owner will let you sam-

ple many of their goods, and it's tempting to ask for one of everything. (Don't actually do this, though—you'd be incapacitated long before you got through their stock.) After fortifying yourself with a sip or two of grappa, head over to the **Torre Belvedere**, an unusual octagonal tower built in the 19th century by the town's mayor.

After this little walk you've earned a great dinner, and next door to the Antica Rosa is a most memorable eatery, the beautiful and elegant **Ristorante Enoteca Boivin**. The staff will discuss wine with you and help you pick a bottle that will go best with your food. (This is where it helps that we're cheapskates who dress *way* down when we travel—no chef or *cameriere* ever recommends a bottle that's out of our price range.) The chef himself comes to the table to describe what he has prepared that evening—all handmade, seasonal, and perfectly prepared. The food is based on Italian cuisine but heavily influenced by culinary traditions from all over the world. In their words, "We are a small restaurant that nevertheless extends its antennas out of its shell as far as possible out into the world." We learn a lot from dining here—about food in general, about wine, about the region, and, most of all, simply about enjoying people and immersing ourselves into a place when we travel.

WHERE TO EAT

Toblino

Castel Toblino
Upscale food presented whimsically and thoughtfully in a beautiful castle setting. A special place to have an unforgettable meal. Closed Tuesdays.
http://www.casteltoblino.com

Route #6 The Trentino

Malgolo

Albergo Ristorante Nerina

Our favorite kind of place to eat: the highest-quality food, sourced locally, presented in a casual, friendly environment. What we wish we could do when we have dinner guests to our own home. Open for lunch and dinner every day.

http://www.albergonerina.it

Trento

Antica Birreria Pedavena

A huge brewery and beer garden with great beer and good pub food. A great way to experience the mix of Italian and Austrian culture in this area. Open every day for lunch and dinner.

http://www.birreriapedavena.com

Levico Terme

Ristorante Enoteca Boivin

Excellent slow food restaurant showcasing the creativity of the inquisitive chef. Cozy and inviting dining room, friendly staff. Open for dinner Tuesday - Sunday, lunch also on the weekends. Closed Monday.

http://www.boivin.it/

Malgolo

Albergo Ristorante Nerina

Family-run hotel and restaurant. Stay here so you can eat here, and in the morning, visit the Eremo Romedio.

http://www.albergonerina.it

Levico Terme

Hotel Antica Rosa
Comfortable hotel right in the center of Levico Terme; parking in the free public lot a few steps away. One room has a teeny balcony with some beautiful views.
http://www.anticarosa.it

Levico Terme

Ponte dei Sapori
Great little shop with wine, cheese, grappa, and specialty products of the region. Free tastes! (within reason) Open every day 8-12:30 and 4-10:30
https://www.ilpontedeisapori.com/

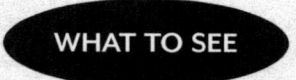

Malgolo

Eremo di San Romedio
Open every day 9-5:30, slightly extended hours in summer. Also, there's a bear!
https://www.visitvaldinon.it/it/da-vedere/arte-e-cultura/santuario-di-san-romedio/

Arco

Castello di Arco
Hours vary by season, so check the link below. Entry 3.50€
https://www.trentino.com/en/highlights/castles/castello-di-arco/

Thun

Castle Thun
Mountaintop castle just north of Trento. 8€/pp entry. Hours vary by season, complete list here:
https://www.buonconsiglio.it/

Trento

Castello di Buonconsiglio
Absolutely incredible, huge castle, plan on at least a 3 hour visit here. Hours vary by season, generally open every day except Monday. 10€/pp entry; don't miss the Torre Aquila for another 2€/pp. Full details here, including combo ticket options:
https://www.buonconsiglio.it/

Sella

Arte Sella
Unique open-air art museum made of wood and stone, in a constant state of change as new artwork is introduced and old artwork is reclaimed by the earth itself. Open every day 10-5, except Christmas. Slightly extended hours in spring, fall, and summer. Entry 8€/pp.
http://www.artesella.it

ROUTE #7

Around Milan-Malpensa Airport

This last route is simple: Drive from your hotel to the airport on your day of departure.

We generally don't care for airport-area lodgings, especially the chain hotels. They're often perfectly clean and reliable, and sometimes they're a necessity based on flight schedules. Still, we find them so devoid of character that we might as well be anywhere in the world. We prefer a place that's unique and interesting, to maximize our travel experience right up to the last possible hour of a trip.

As **Milan-Malpensa airport (MXP)** is the most common airport to fly into and out of when visiting Italy's lakes, we've made a point of finding interesting places to stay on our last night that are within an hour's drive. Following are just two of our favorites. They illustrate the kind of places we try to find for ourselves and our clients.

Vigevano: This is a large, sprawling town, and not terribly attractive on the outskirts. But its old *centro* is rich with interesting things to do and see. The central *piazza* is huge and striking, often filled with vendors' stalls for market days or for the town's annual **Chocolate Festival**. At one end

stands the monumental **Cattedrale di Santi Ambrogio e Carlo**, dating from the 16th century but with sections going back many centuries before. At the other end is the entrance to the **Castello Sforzesco** complex, a series of buildings including a climbable clock tower, a hidden, medieval *strada coperta* ("covered road"), a museum dedicated to Leonardo da Vinci, and the fun and quirky **International Shoe Museum**. The latter features shoes

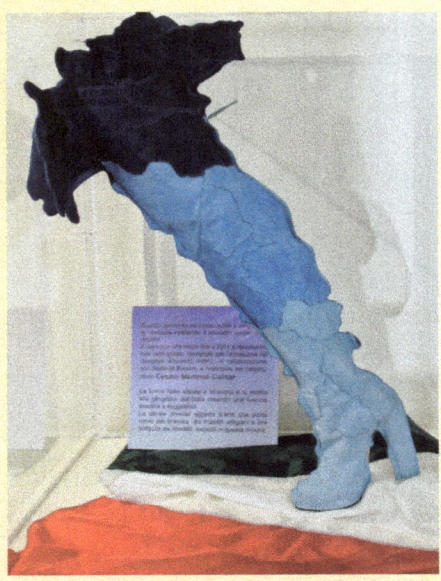

from several centuries and from multiple cultures. You'll find the shoes of the Pope here, and also those of ... Shaquille O'Neal? The town is known for cuisine based on goose, which is the specialty of **L'Oca Ciuca** on the other side of the castle. A block from the *piazza* is the cozy **Locanda San Bernardo**, with free enclosed (off-street) parking and gracious hosts.

Vigevano is about 45 minutes from MXP, and it's also a good place to stop on your way from touring the Emilia-Romagna region to the south.

For a much closer ride to the airport, check out **Osteria dello Sperone**, just 10 minutes away from MXP. You'll never know you're that close, though: This place is a tiny pocket of paradise on the Fiume Ticino. Remember that river from Route 2, at the south end of Lago Maggiore? Here it flows noisily next to a natural park and wildlife area, totally

Route #7 Around Milan-Malpensa Airport

obscuring any sounds of the airplanes coming and going just a few kilometers away. Marina and her family staff offer home cooking and gregarious service at the on-site restaurant.

Within routes 1 and 2, you'll also find that several other towns and lodgings we recommend lie within an hour or so of MXP, so be smart when planning a trip to these lakes. Your last night in Italy can absolutely be as memorable as the rest of your trip!

Vigevano

L'Oca Ciuca
Specializing in a local delicacy—goose. Large outdoor terrace for warmer months. Fresh bread and pastries made on premises. Closed Wednesdays.

http://www.locaciuca.com/

Lonate Pozzolo

Osteria della Sperone
Unbelievably affordable B&B just 10 minutes from Milan's airport, in a quiet corner of the countryside. Good family-run restaurant on the ground floor.

https://www.facebook.com/osteriadellosperone/

Vigevano

Locanda San Bernardo
Cute B&B a couple of blocks from the town's main square, free internal secured parking, large rooms.

https://www.locandasanbernardo.it

Route #7 Around Milan-Malpensa Airport

Vigevano

International Shoe Museum
A fun, quirky, extensive museum, located in the Castello Sforzesco complex. Free entry.
http://www.museocalzaturavigevano.it

APPENDIX 1

The Restaurant Experience

There are a lot of differences between eating in Italy and eating in the States. Here are a few tips on what to expect, and how to enjoy the dining experience to its fullest.

Restaurants have many names in Italy: *Ristorante, Osteria, Trattoria,* and *Locanda* are by far the most common.

The first thing that will happen at any restaurant is the *cameriere* bringing bread and asking what kind of *acqua* (water) you would like. This will always be bottled water, and can be *naturale* (flat) or *frizzante/gassata* (sparkling). Don't ask for tap water—this would be like asking for a drink out of the garden hose.

Bread will usually not come with butter or a dish of oil; it is meant to be used to soak up sauces on your plates. You'll see that a per-person *coperto* (cover charge) is indicated on the menu. This is typically a couple of bucks, and is meant to stand as a minimum service charge.

Meals are served in courses:

Antipasti - appetizers

Primi - pastas, soups or *risotto*

Secondi - meat dishes—this will be just meat; if you want a side dish, order a contorni

Contorni - vegetables, potatoes or salad

Dolci - desserts; occasionally this list will include a cheese plate

Cafe/digestivi - coffee (don't get a cappuccino!) or digestive liqueur, like an *amaro* or a *grappa*

Diners are not obligated or expected to order a dish from every course; we frequently skip either the pasta or the meat course. However, if you find yourself in an especially charming or romantic location, settle in for what we refer to as an "epic" meal.

Once you have a table, it's yours for the night. There will be no turnover or pressure for you to leave. It's generally considered very rude to put a bill on the table, so often the service staff is waiting for you at the end of a meal to approach them to ask for *il conto* (the bill).

Meals are slow, and there can be a good amount of time in between courses, as they are making your dish from scratch. If you want a faster meal, try a *panificio* (sandwich shop), pizzeria, or bar, or grab a picnic lunch at a grocery store.

Most small-town restaurants are family-owned, and as a result they won't always adhere to their stated schedules. If one of their family members has a baby or a sudden medical need/wedding/vacation, they might not open up as usual. Be ready to improvise.

A note on tipping

After a meal, you'll need to ask for *il conto* (the check), as they won't try to bum-rush you out as they do in the States. Though it's not generally expected, we often leave a little something extra — usually somewhere between 10 and 20 percent — to show appreciation for good service.

Meal times and reservations

While reservations are not generally required, it's a good idea to have them, even in casual restaurants. Reservations can be made the same day, even an hour in advance. Basically you are just reserving a table and getting a head-start on the lunch rush. No ties/jackets are ever required at the places we recommend (though you are welcome to wear them if you like). Some of the restaurants we recommend are real mom-and-pop places, and some are upscale, but all will allow you to eat there wearing regular clothing (no Speedos/flip flops, however).

It's not unusual to make a reservation and then be the only people eating that day. Sometimes the reservation just insures that the restaurant opens at all. In the US if you saw an empty restaurant, you'd know that was a sign of poor quality; but that is often not true in Italy, especially in very small towns. No reservations are required (or even possible) in pizzerias and small sandwich shops; reservations are only for sit-down restaurants.

Seatings for *pranzo* (lunch) generally happen no earlier than 12:30 and no later than maybe 2:00. Shoot for 1:00-1:30 to be safe. If you're looking for a place to eat at 2:30, you may be totally out of luck.

Cena (dinner) starts at maybe 7:30, and goes on until everyone is done eating. Again, if you wait much later than 9:00, they may turn you away, depending on how busy the place is.

Breakfasts: Some lodgings offer *colazione* (breakfast), which range from a full-service spread of meats, cheeses, fruits and breads to a packet of biscuits and a yogurt cup in the mini-fridge. We almost always skip it altogether; we like to say that if you need breakfast, you didn't do dinner right.

Bar Culture

Italy's main social scene is at the various neighborhood or roadside bars. This is where you get your coffee in the morning (or any time of day, really), your *aperitivo* before lunch, your drinks and such before or after dinner. Ask for a *café* and you'll get the tiny, very strong espresso. *Cappuccino*, with its frothy steamed milk on top, is typical in the mornings only, though they will make you one any time. Sometimes they will shorten the word "cappuccino" to the slang "cappucci".

Other common drinks

Spritz Aperol (sweeter) or *Spritz Campari* (more bitter) are cocktails with prosecco, campari, and soda; *spremuta* (fresh squeezed orange juice, you'll see a machine behind the bar with a basket of oranges if they have this); *café corretto* (espresso mixed with grappa); prosecco; and of course wine. At the bar you can also buy a bottle of water (*naturale* or *frizzante*), which you can drink there or take on the road.

We've never seen anyone drinking cocktails like a martini or a cosmopolitan, though they could probably make one if requested. In the last few years many bars have begun to offer Italian-made *birra artigianale*—artisanal beers.

The bar is a great place to try a shot of the endless varieties of Italian 'amari', or liqueurs. Ask for "*un amaro*", and just point to the one you'd like to try. Cynar (CHEE-nar) is made from artichokes, Montenegro from herbs, Averna also from herbs... It can be fun to give them a try, each will cost 2-4€. They will probably ask you if you want it with ice ("*con ghiaccio*").

If you order a cocktail (e.g. Aperol spritz, or an *amaro*), the bartender may also bring you a little dish of nuts or olives, tiny sandwich bites or other snacks. Those are free with your drink. If you're happy with the drink and service, it's nice to leave a Euro or two as a tip. (Note: baristas do not generally expect tips, but they always appreciate one.)

Key dining terms

Per favore, grazie — please, thank you (Use these regularly!)

colazione, pranzo, cena — breakfast, lunch, dinner

prenotazione — reservation

tavola — dining table

carta — menu

aperitivo — a little drink before the meal

vino della casa — house wine

bicchiere — glass

bottiglia — bottle

carafe — carafe

barriche — barrel

fuori/dentro — outside/inside ("*Possiamo mangiare fuori?*" "Can we eat outside?")

digestivo — a little drink after the meal

Fatto in casa — made in-house

troppo cibo — too much food

sono pieno — I am full

non posso mangiare piu — I can't eat any more

OK, forse solo uno dolce, per favore — okay, maybe just one dessert, please

APPENDIX 2
GENERAL TIPS FOR TRAVELING IN ITALY

Passports

Your US passport must be valid for six months after the last date of your trip. If your passport expires in October and your trip ends in May, you will not be able to board the plane.

If you need a new passport or need to renew your old one, the State Department recommends doing that at least 6 weeks in advance. We recommend 3 months, just to avoid the stress of frantically checking the mail every day. We also highly recommend applying for Global Entry, which will greatly expedite your time waiting in line at both ends of your trip.

Renting a car

International Driver's Licenses are required for foreign drivers in Italy. These can be purchased at AAA (even for nonmembers) for $15. You will also need your regular driver's license.

Snow tires or chains are now legally required between November 15 and April 15. This will often mean an additional fee from the rental company (to hire chains) if the car is not equipped with snow tires. You may not see any snow (we rarely have, after multiple winter trips) but nevertheless you are required to pay to be prepared. If you know it is going to snow, or if it starts to snow, you need to stop and get the chains on. Having not put chains on a car since 1980 or so, we don't love the idea either, but it's a small price to pay for a great trip (and to avoid a citation from the *Carabinieri*, the Italian state police). For more driving tips — from picking up the car to insurance to traffic signs to navigation to parking — check our website, http://www.LittleRoadsEurope.com, which includes many pictures and links.

Driving in Italy

People are often intimidated by driving in Italy. The drivers are often fast and aggressive, and American drivers may feel pressured to go faster by drivers who tailgate very closely. This is just a cultural norm in Italy—remember that it's not personal. If someone is following you too closely, look ahead for a place to pull over and let them pass easily. Usually they're not even paying attention to you, they just drive like this out of habit. If they are irritated at your slow speed, that's okay—once they pass you, you'll probably never have to see them again. Give them a little wave and cheerful *"Ciao!"* as they pass you by.

Tolls

The only toll roads are the Autostrada highways. Approaching a toll plaza, you'll see lanes marked in blue that say "*Carte*" (credit cards). You can use your credit card in the automated machines to get through. If you prefer to pay cash, look for the lanes marked with the pictures of money. Some of the toll plazas give you a "*biglietto*"—a ticket, like on the NJ Turnpike—upon exiting, you insert that before inserting your *carta* (credit card) to pay the toll.

Gas Stations

Filling up is usually easy enough, at one of the many service stations along the highways or in towns. Many of them have two lanes, one for "*Servizio*" and one "*Fai da te*" (do-it-yourself). The self-service is a little cheaper, but we usually opt for the service attendant in case there's some trick to the pumps. Ask for "*senza piombo*" (unleaded) or "*diesel*" (diesel), and tell him how much you want—a number of euro, or just "*al pieno*" (full). (And don't forget to say "*per favore*"!) If the weather is bad we usually tip the attendant a couple of bucks. Most of these places take credit cards, and you'll have to go inside their little office to pay. Sometimes the place is set up just like an American convenience store—just note the number of your pump and tell the clerks inside, and they'll ring you up.

Note: On Sundays, many if not all service stations are closed. In this event, some of them have auto-pay machines that take cash and, depending on the specific machine, some types of cards. These can be confusing, and for this reason we always avoid them altogether, making sure that on Saturday we have a full tank.

Money

Cash is still king. Nearly all restaurants and hotels accept credit cards, but some still do not, so make sure you know before you buy. Bars will usually not accept cards, and certainly not for a *conto* of just a few bucks — you will always need cash for that. Italians also have a deep love for exact change, and efforts on your part to produce exact change will be appreciated. They also have a love of small bills. Trying to buy a 1€ espresso with a 20€ note will garner you some dirty looks, and in small towns, they may not even have enough change for that.

Note: We've found that many places that do accept cards do not accept American Express, since their commission fees are so high. Mastercard and VISA are generally fine.

Check with your bank about international

ATM withdrawal fees. We use the *bancomat*—ATM—there as needed, as the exchange rate is the same or close to what you will find at the airport. (Traveler's checks have gone the way of wooden dentures, so don't even ask.)

Exchange counters at the airport often offer "deals" that allow you to exchange unspent Euros on your trip back without fees. Alternatively, you can just keep track of your spending in general and work your way down to zero Euros at the end of your trip. Or stash it away for your next trip!

Wi-Fi

Free wi-fi is available at many B&Bs, restaurants and bars. You can call your phone company and have an international data package added for a month. That said, we recommend just using free wi-fi when you find it, or better yet, take a break from constantly being tethered to your phone. You'll be amazed at how much more you experience things around you when you are not focused on staring at a small screen.

Packing

It's impossible to overstate the value of packing light for a good trip, for two reasons: 1) You want the most mobility and flexibility, so your focus is on experiencing the place you are visiting, and not managing the mound of stuff in your suitcase; and 2) the goal is to arrive with very little, and leave with bags laden down with all the goodies you'll find. Trust us, you'll be disappointed if you can't buy that bottle of oil or ceramic vase because you had to make room for your hairdryer/extra shoes/umbrella. This is especially important on a trip to the Italian lakes if you're heading for lodgings on one of the islands (e.g., Isola Pescatori on Lake Maggiore, Monte Isola on Lake Iseo)—you'll want to have no more than a little bag to carry onto the boat for your island getaway.

We've traveled overseas dozens of times, and we offer extensive advice on packing smart on our website, http://www.LittleRoadsEurope.com.

Language

Even in small towns you will often find plenty of English-speakers. Oftentimes you'll find people who want to practice their English by chatting with you. That said, we highly recommend starting your encounters with a bit of Italian. A simple *"buon giorno"* (good day), *"per favore"* (please), or *"grazie"* (thank you) goes a long way. It's easy to learn a few key phrases, and making the effort opens the door for making real connections with people. It's also important to remember that you are a guest in their country, and to treat people the way you would like to be treated.

A note on Visiting/Opening Hours

Opening hours for shops and sites are variable according to the season; but in general, most sites are open from mid-morning until lunchtime, and then reopen from the mid-afternoon until early evening. For most tourist sites (e.g., museums, castles), the last entry is 30-45 minutes before the actual closing time.

On festival days (of which there are many), shops and other businesses may be closed, but most tourist sites will be open (perhaps with varying hours). Look for paper signs plastered on walls for information that you'd normally expect to find on a website; while web presence is increasing, roadside flyers are still the most common form of advertising.

Lodging — What to Expect, What to Look For

Lodging in Italy is much less of the cookie-cutter experience you'll find in the US. In the large Italian cities you can find standard and also luxurious hotels that are like any you would find around the globe. In the smaller towns, though, chain hotels are nonexistent. Instead you'll find small, family run hotels and B&Bs. Sometimes a hotel will be called "Albergo", "Pensione", or "Locanda". A locanda is usually a hotel with a restaurant. B&Bs usually mean you'll have breakfast included, but that breakfast will never involve the eggs, waffles, bacon, and cinnamon buns that you would find at an American B&B. Italians eat very light breakfasts — we always say that if you need breakfast, you didn't do dinner right. At a typical B&B breakfast you'll find coffee, juice, breads (fresh or packaged) and jams, nutella, and maybe yogurt. We almost always skip these breakfasts and instead opt to eat at a nearby bar with the locals, where we take in the sights, smells and sounds of the day. If you intend to eat hotel breakfast, be sure to check if your B&B or hotel offers it free — sometimes there is an additional charge.

A few other things you likely won't find in a small town Italian hotel:

- hairdryers, irons and ironing boards, coffee service, room service
- mini fridge (though these are becoming more common now, to our delight)
- TV and phone
- Air conditioning
- elevators
- large, nearby parking lots
- 24 hour concierge

Some of these may be there, but they are not ubiquitous as in American hotels.

You *will* find:
- religious art on the walls
- proprietors who live there or quite nearby, and know the area well
- stunning views
- peace and quiet

When we look for lodging, we are always looking for location. Sometimes we'll book a remote castle, which is not near any restaurants — in that case we may have picnic dinners to avoid driving at night, and also to spend the most time possible in a stunning fairytale location. Sometimes we'll book into a restaurant that has rooms upstairs, so we can eat "epic" meals and then roll ourselves up the stairs at the end of the night to sleep it off. Most often we book small, affordable places in or within walking distance to small walled towns, so we can park the car and leave it while we explore the town on foot. We always look for places that are going to give us a memorable, meaningful trip with a minimum of hassle.

A planning note

Many of the small places we list in this book are, to our knowledge, not listed anywhere else. We have made every effort to accumulate and update the information in this book; however, small businesses can shut down or be closed unexpectedly for illnesses, vacations (*"ferie"*), or just because they felt like it. Many of the places we list have websites and/or Facebook pages; we suggest you confirm their opening days/times before visiting to avoid disappointment. Without limit, we are not responsible for any distress, disappointment, or damage incurred by following this guide. However, if you do find information that you think could use updating, please let us know by contacting us via email at littleroadseurope@gmail.com.

Buon appetitio, e buon viaggio!

Thank you!

We hope you've enjoyed this book. For more information on the places we travel, please visit us at **www.LittleRoadsEurope.com**.

Interested in other parts of Europe? Check out our other Little Roads Europe Travel Guides, our award-winning, small-town foodie guidebooks to Italy, in which we explore the breadbasket of **Emilia-Romagna** and the iconic cuisine of **Tuscany**. Find out how we apply our travel philosophy to exploring these beautiful regions of Italy, visiting its historic small towns, and of course eating its famously fantastic food. Or take a look at our guide to **Ireland**, and discover all the "Little Roads" secrets of the Emerald Isle!

If you're thinking about a trip to Ireland or Italy, we hope you'll consider our **Itinerary-Building Service**. We design custom itineraries for clients based on our extensive travel experiences in Ireland and the northern regions of Italy. Working from your preferences, we'll help you navigate these regions, make reservations, visit artisans, and give recommendations for a trip that is authentic, immersive, memorable and affordable. Start your vacation before you even leave, and let us do the hard part!

- Zeneba & Matt

Little Roads Europe Travel Guide Series

2015, 2016, 2017   2015, 2016, 2017

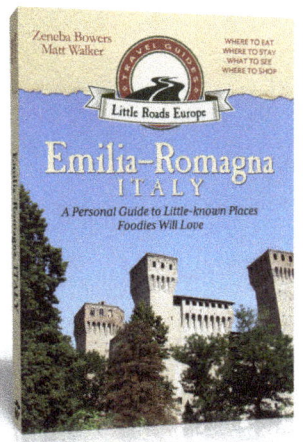

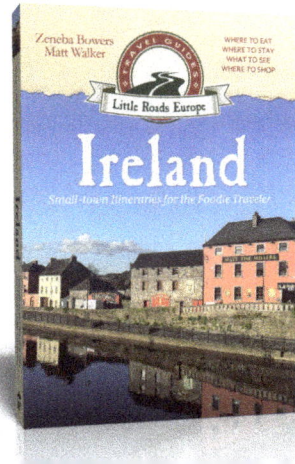

www.ingramcontent.com/pod-product-compliance
Lightning Source LLC
Chambersburg PA
CBHW041312110526
44591CB00022B/2891